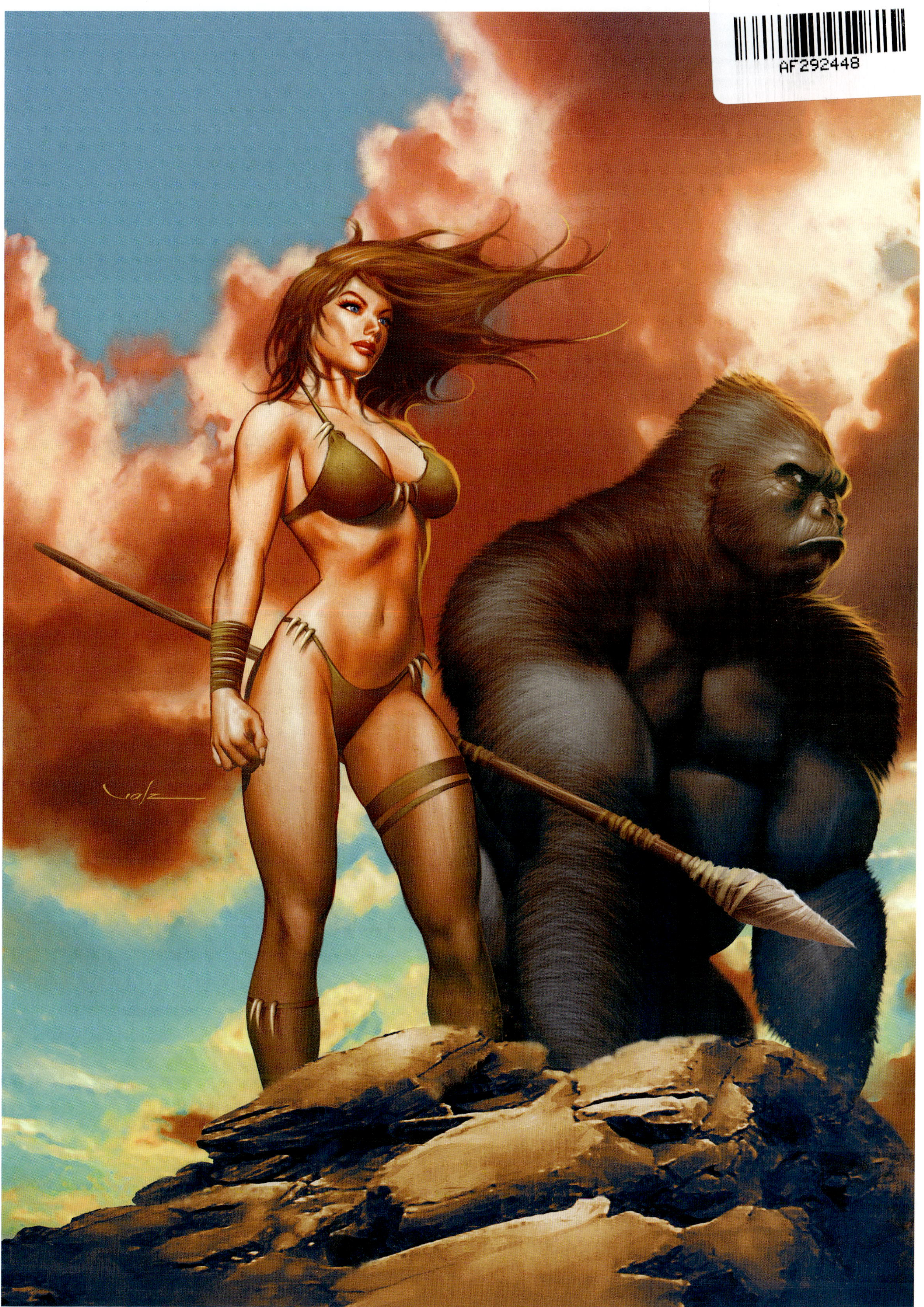

Savage World

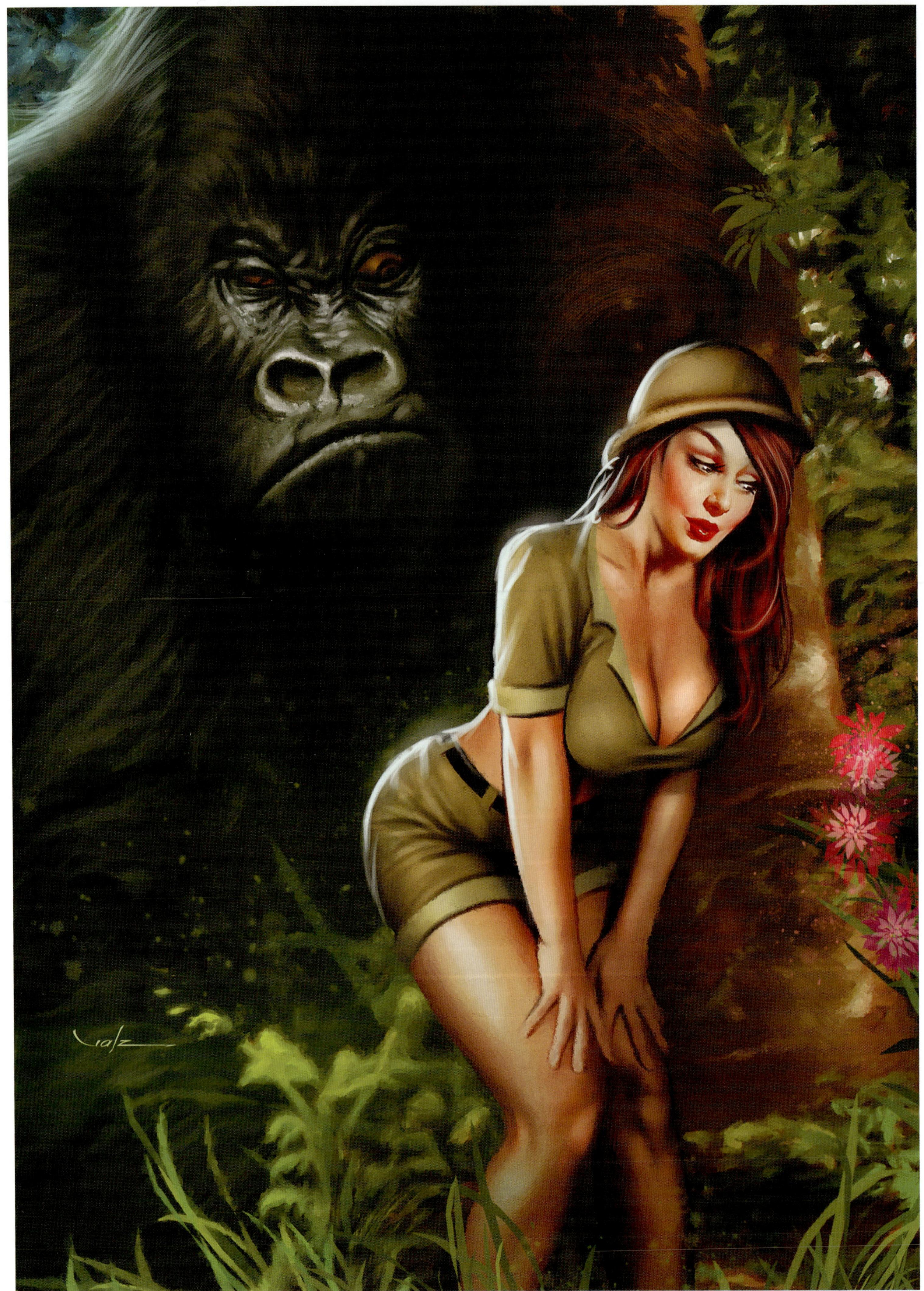

A Nice View

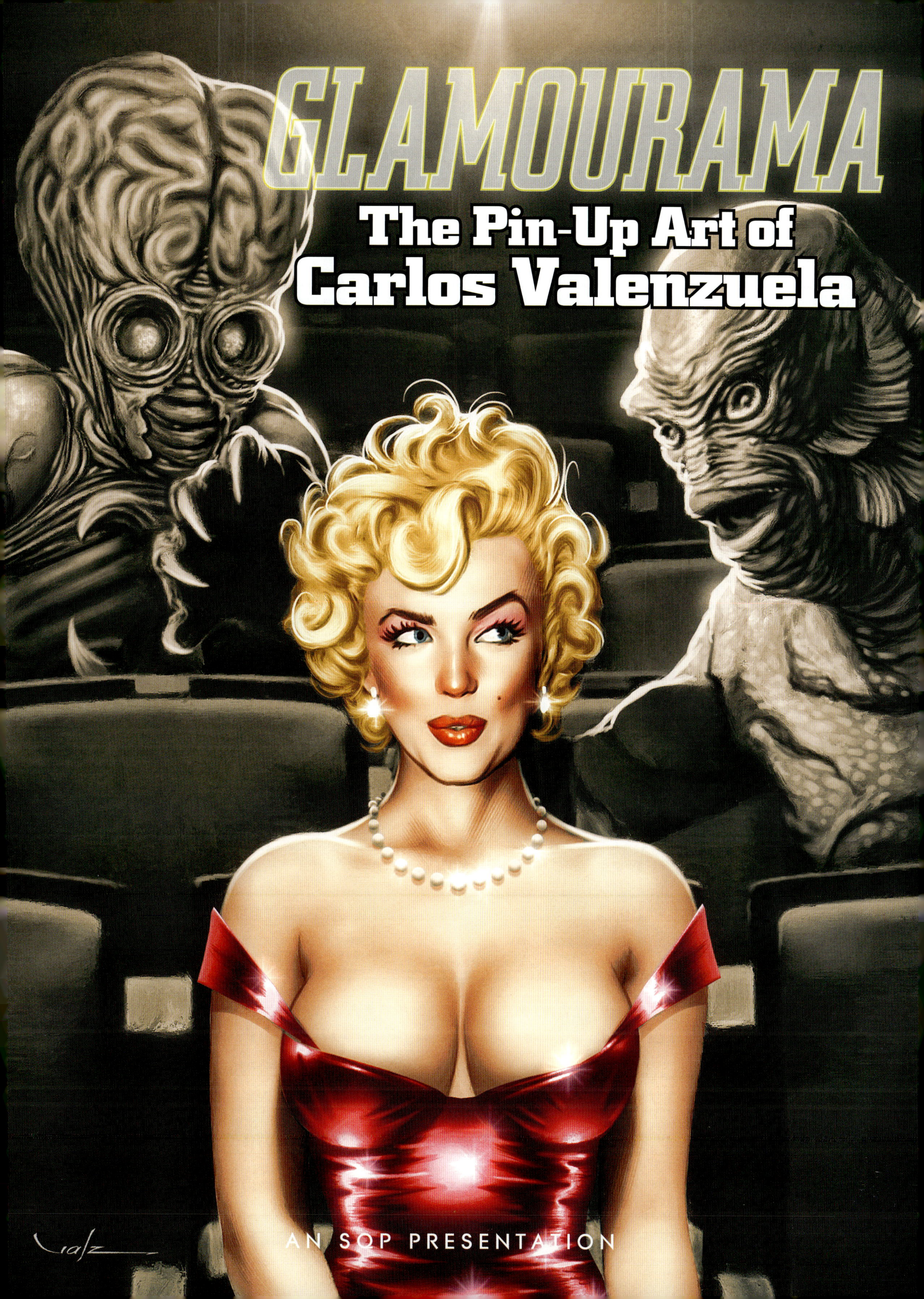

GLAMOURAMA
The Pin-Up Art of
Carlos Valenzuela
AN SOP PRESENTATION

Retro-Active!
Illustrator Carlos Valenzuela Gets his Blasts from the Past!

Every time I look through my portfolio I'm convinced I'm living in the wrong age.

I've always been fascinated by all things 50's - movies, art, fashion styles, women, etc, and that reflects a lot in my work. I can't deny the power of that age's influence, even if I look to those times through impossibly nostalgic eyes (my birth certificate **DOES** say I was born in 1975).

Naturally, I grew up watching a lot of sci-fi and horror movies (the classics are **still** the best), and of course, reading comic books. My not-so-secret origin story would start the day I realized I could grab a pencil and do my **own** stories and characters! From that point on, there was no stopping me! Then I discovered the works of Frank Frazetta, Moebius and Rich Corben, and decided that I would be a fantasy illustrator.

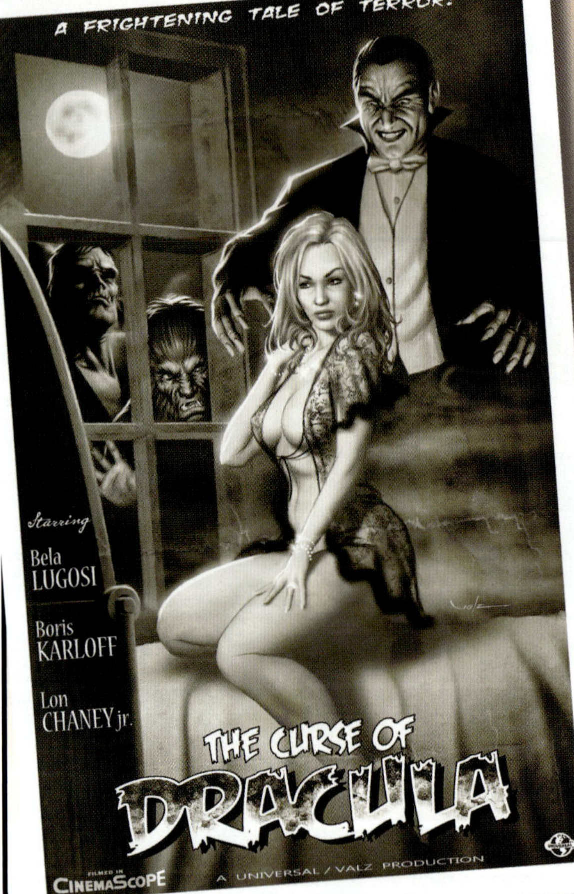

As to the main subject of my works, let's face it, there is nothing more beautiful than the female form.
The curves – the shapes - the allure. Women are simply nature's most intoxicating invention!
And for all its political "incorrectness" - the damsel in distress is **always** a solid favorite, and the one most clients tend to ask me for. Beautiful and glamorous ladies in danger, fighting some strange creatures or a mad scientist, was what **sold** pulp magazines and fiction back in the good old days, so it's a trip for me to visit that retro "classic" style (with my own modern twist, of course).

In this volume of "**Glamourama**", you'll see my love of Hollywood honeys and classic movie monsters, sci-fi femmes and Hammer horror queens, lady vampires and creatures that go "rub" in the night! It's all the guilty pleasures that make life (and the undead) worthwhile!

Enjoy!

Carlos Valenzuela
May 2013

ABOUT THE ARTIST

Carlos Valenzuela is a professional illustrator and comic book artist from Chile. He's worked for several companies in the entertainment field like Fantasy Flight Games, SQP Art Books, Comics Buyer's Guide, Pyranha Bytes, Avatar Press, Arcana Comics, Ballistic Publishing, Ilex UK, IDW Publishing, etc. doing book cover illustrations, posters, interior book art and artwork for collective card games and comic books.
Has also worked as a cover artist for IDW Publishing (X-Files, Mars Attacks) and has done poster and art prints for Under The Floorboards (UK)

Since 1973, showcasing the very finest in fantasy, erotic, & pin-up illustration.

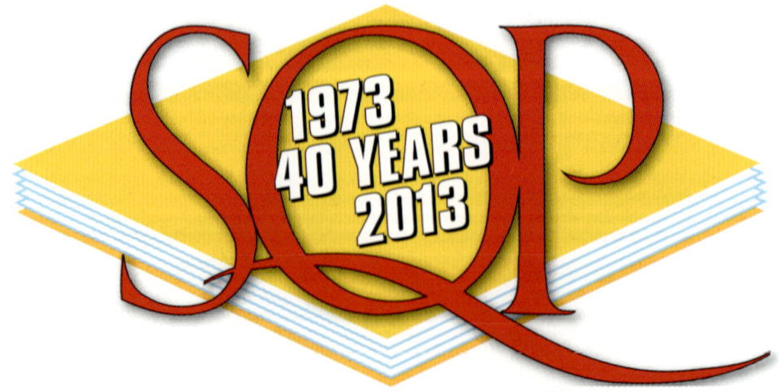

www.sqpartbooks.com

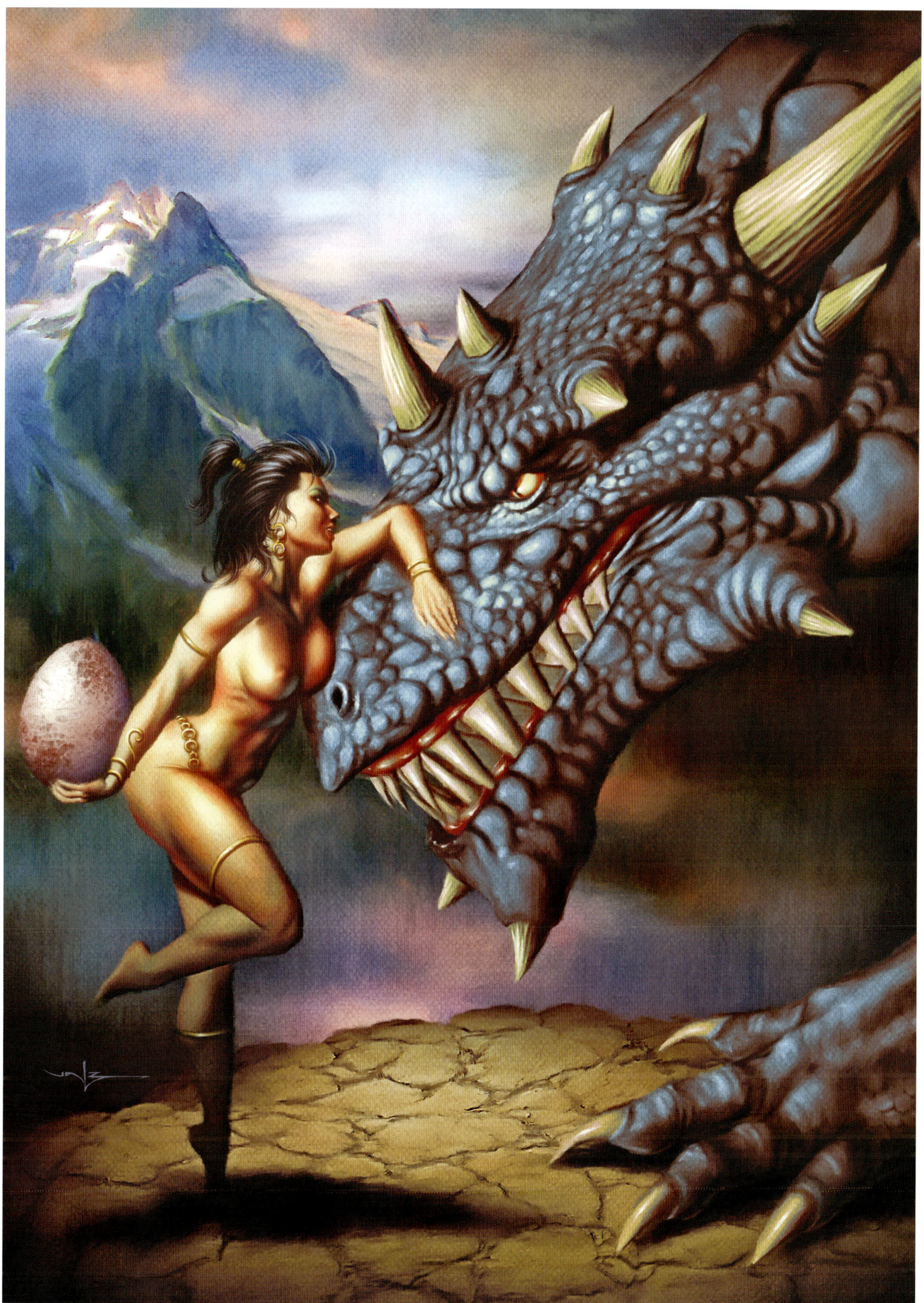

The Thief

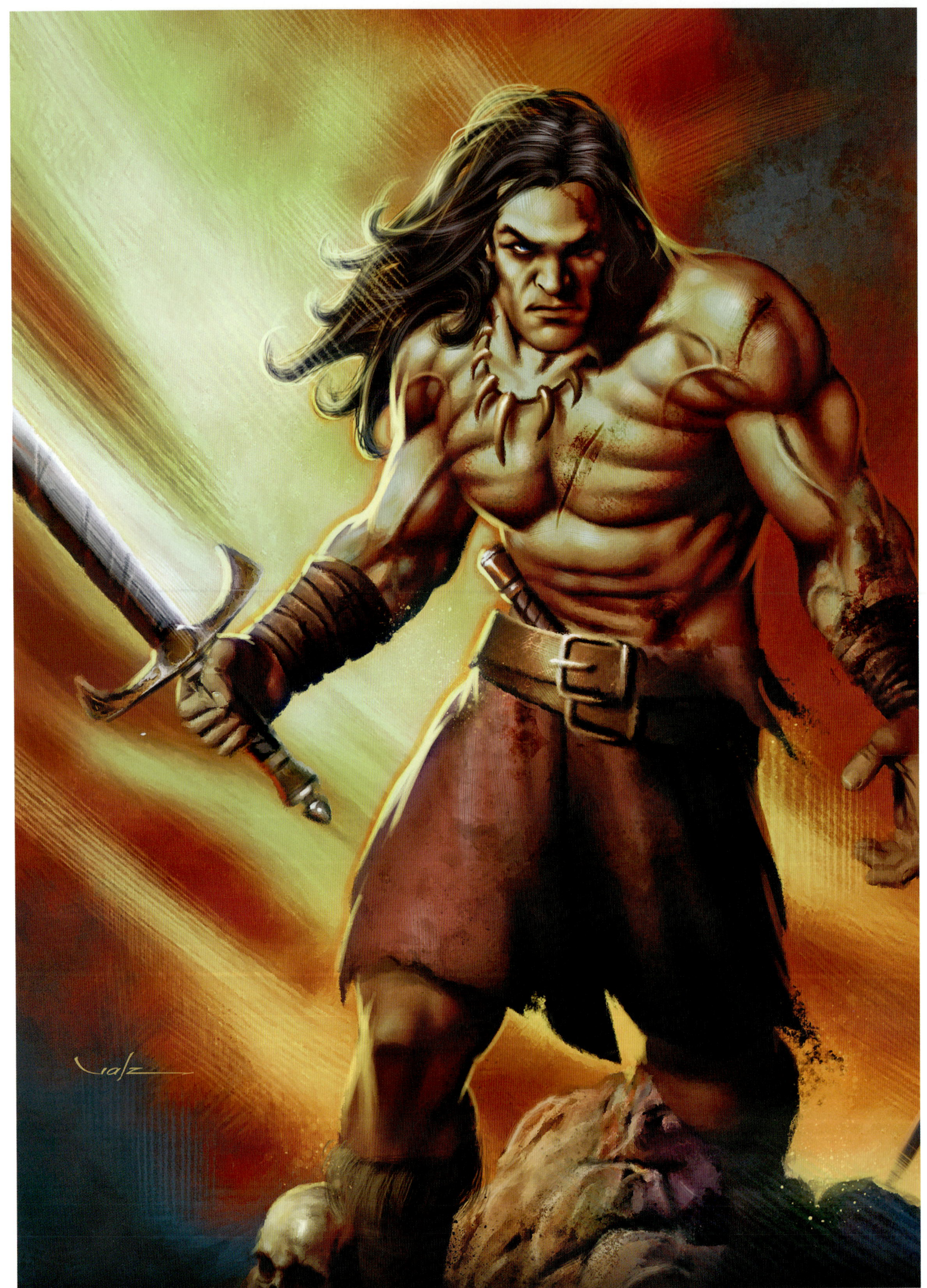

The Warrior

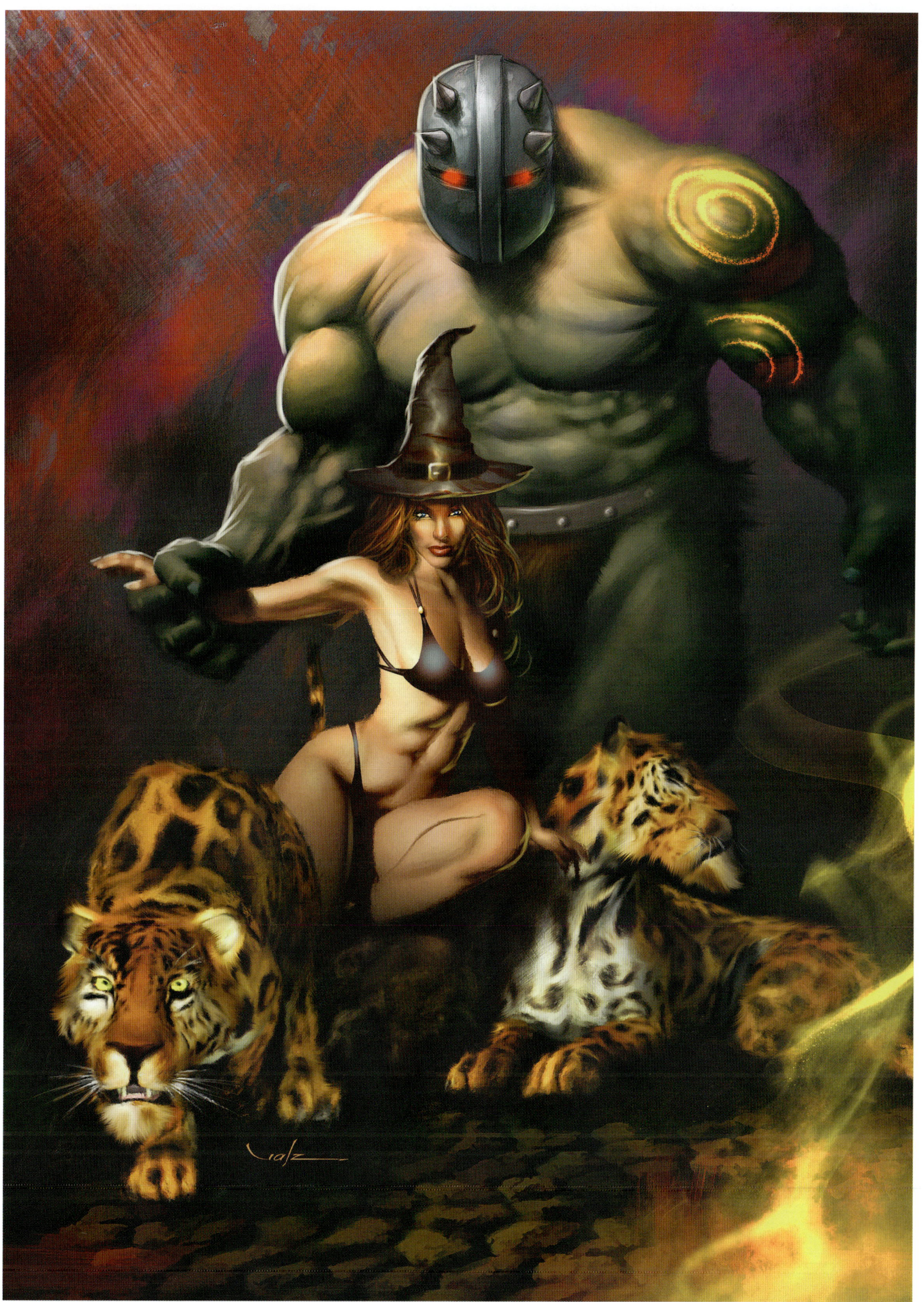

Beauty And Friends

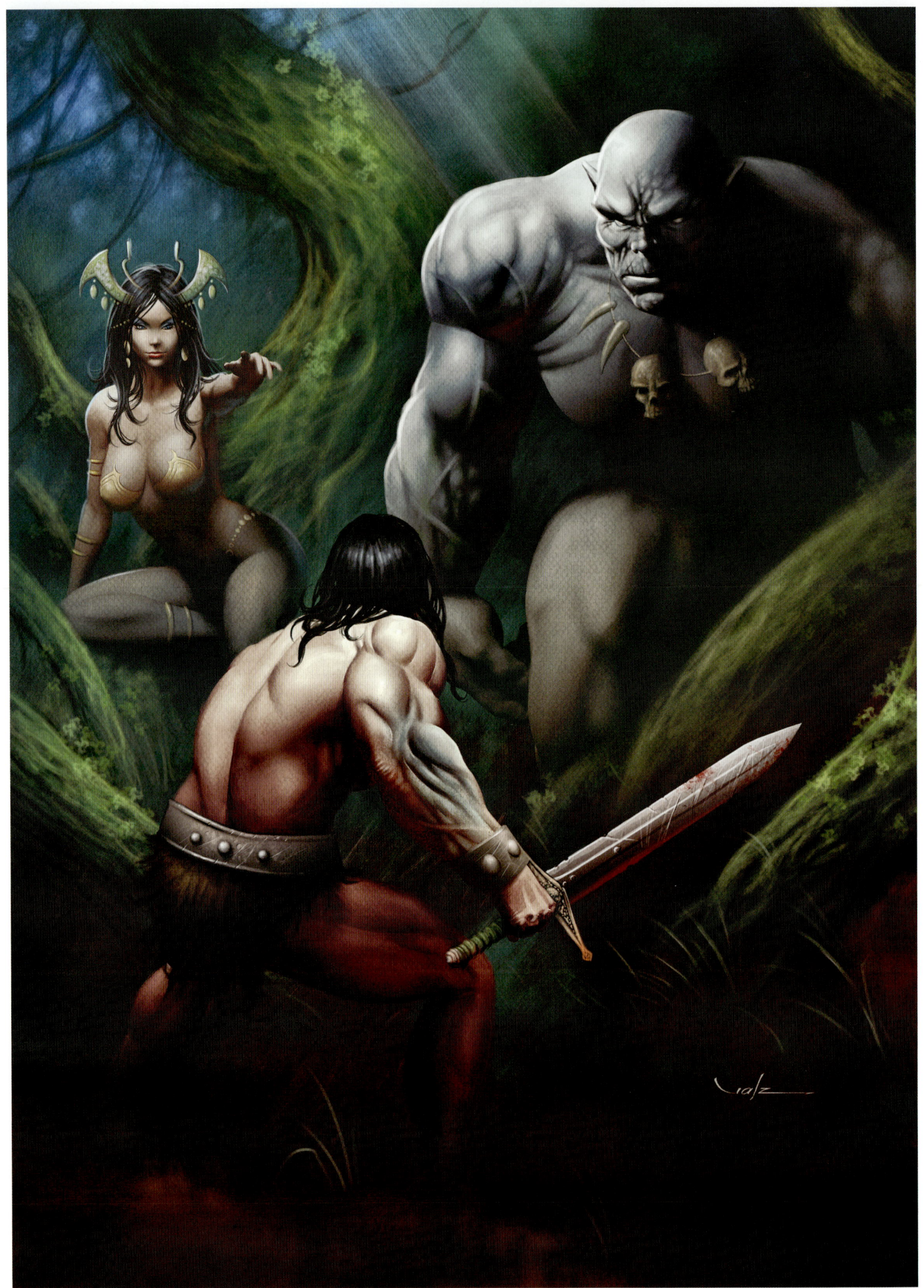

THE TRAP

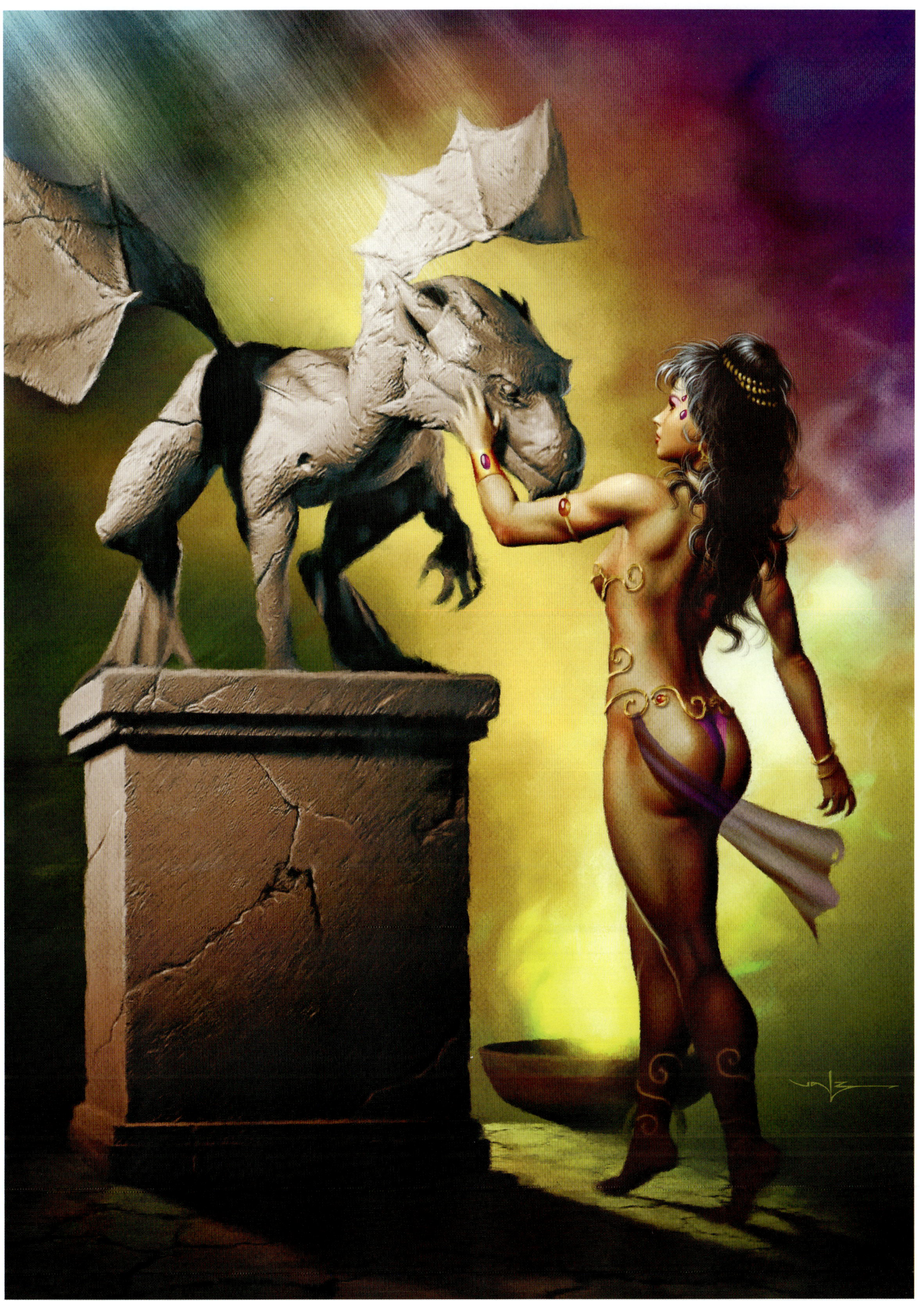

Stroking The Past

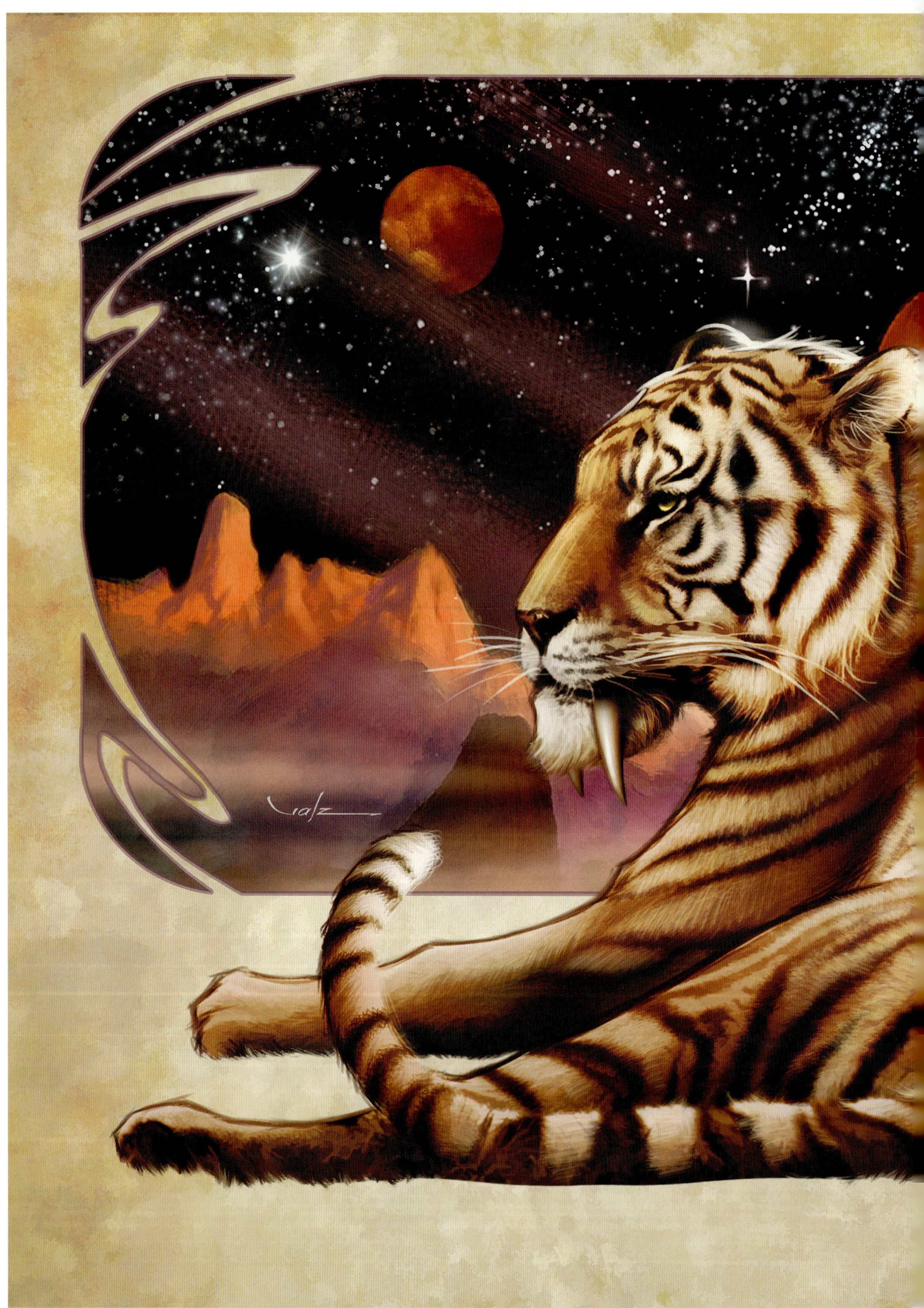

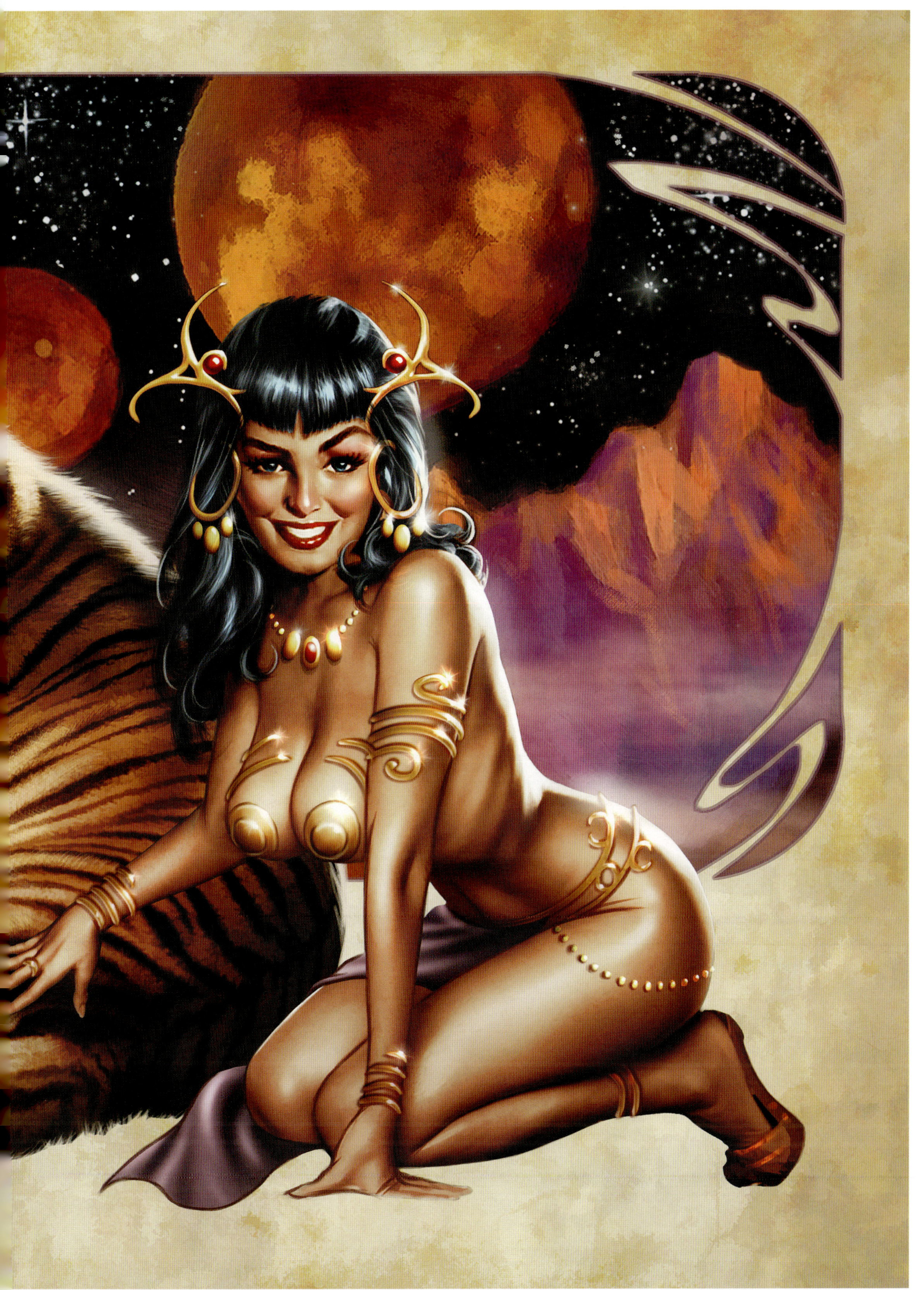

Martian Slave

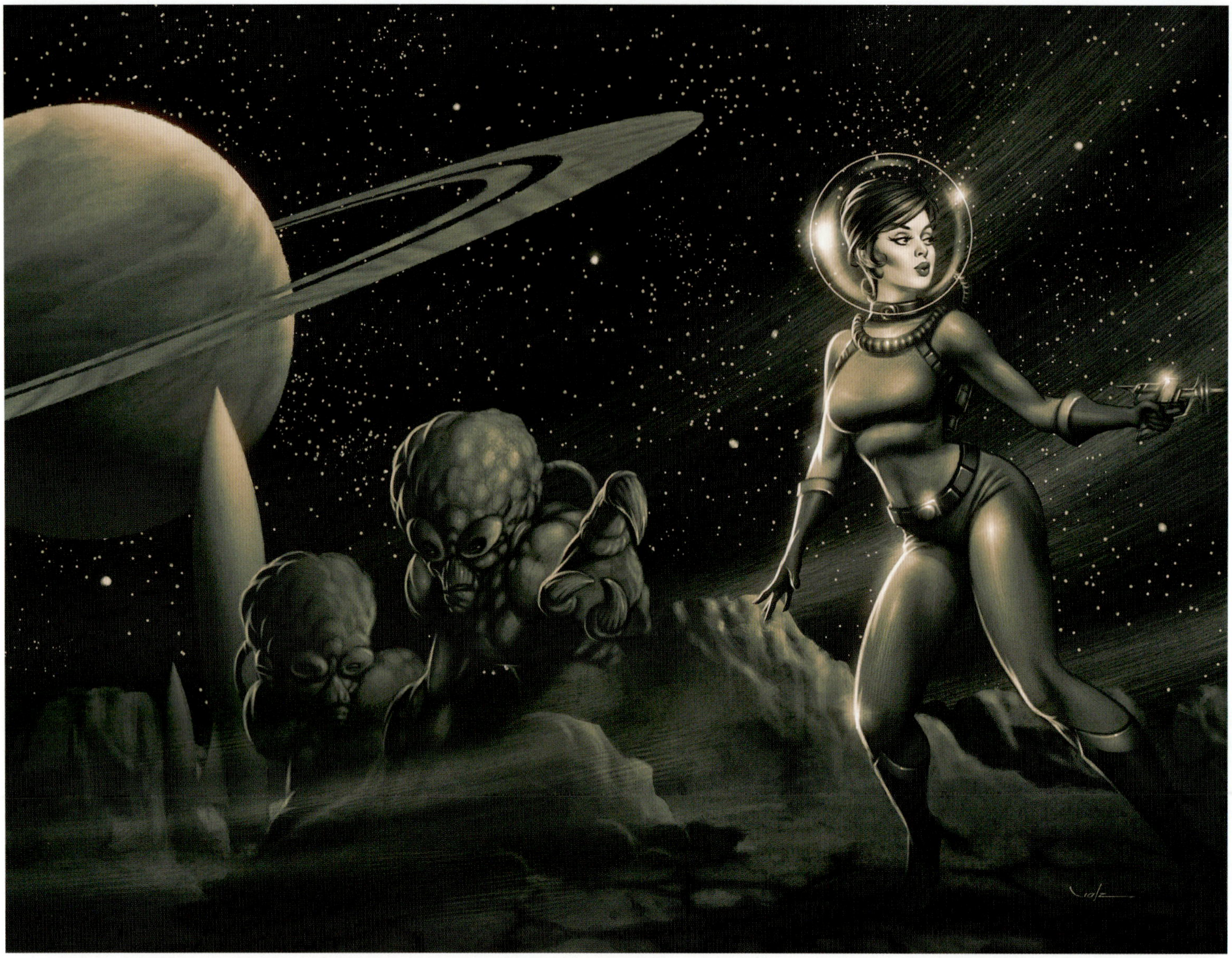

Dangerous Planet

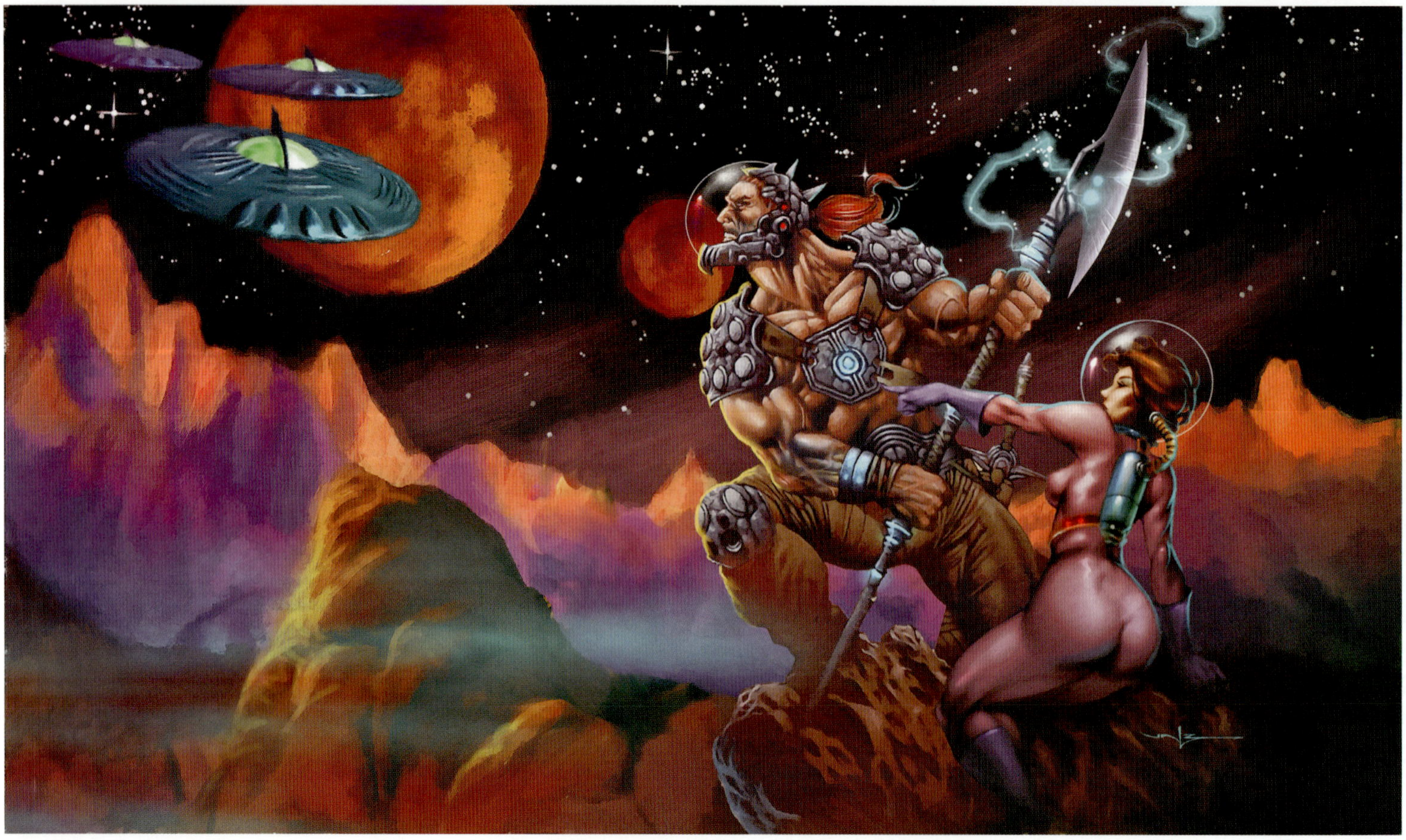

Invaders On Mars

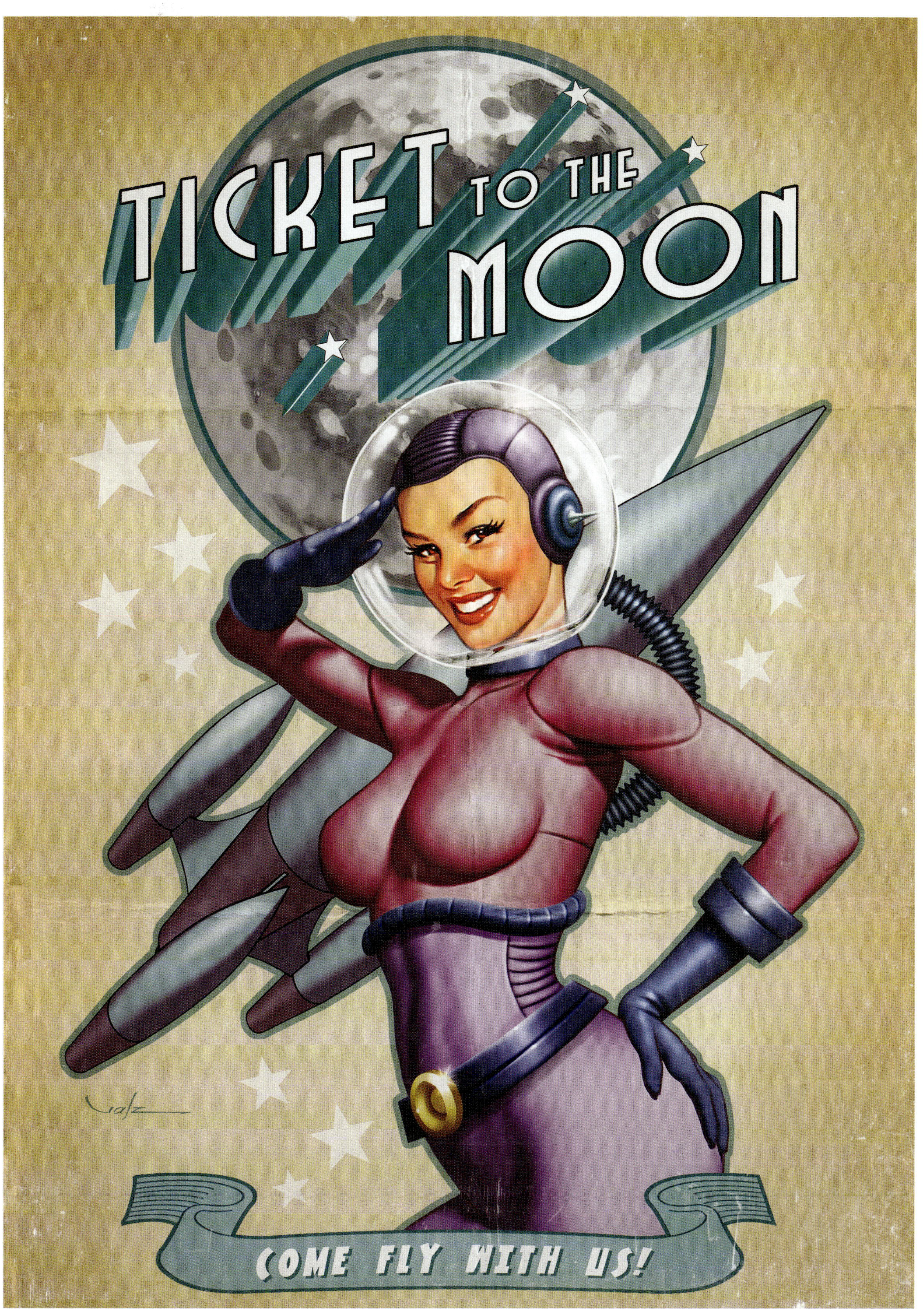

Ticket To The Moon

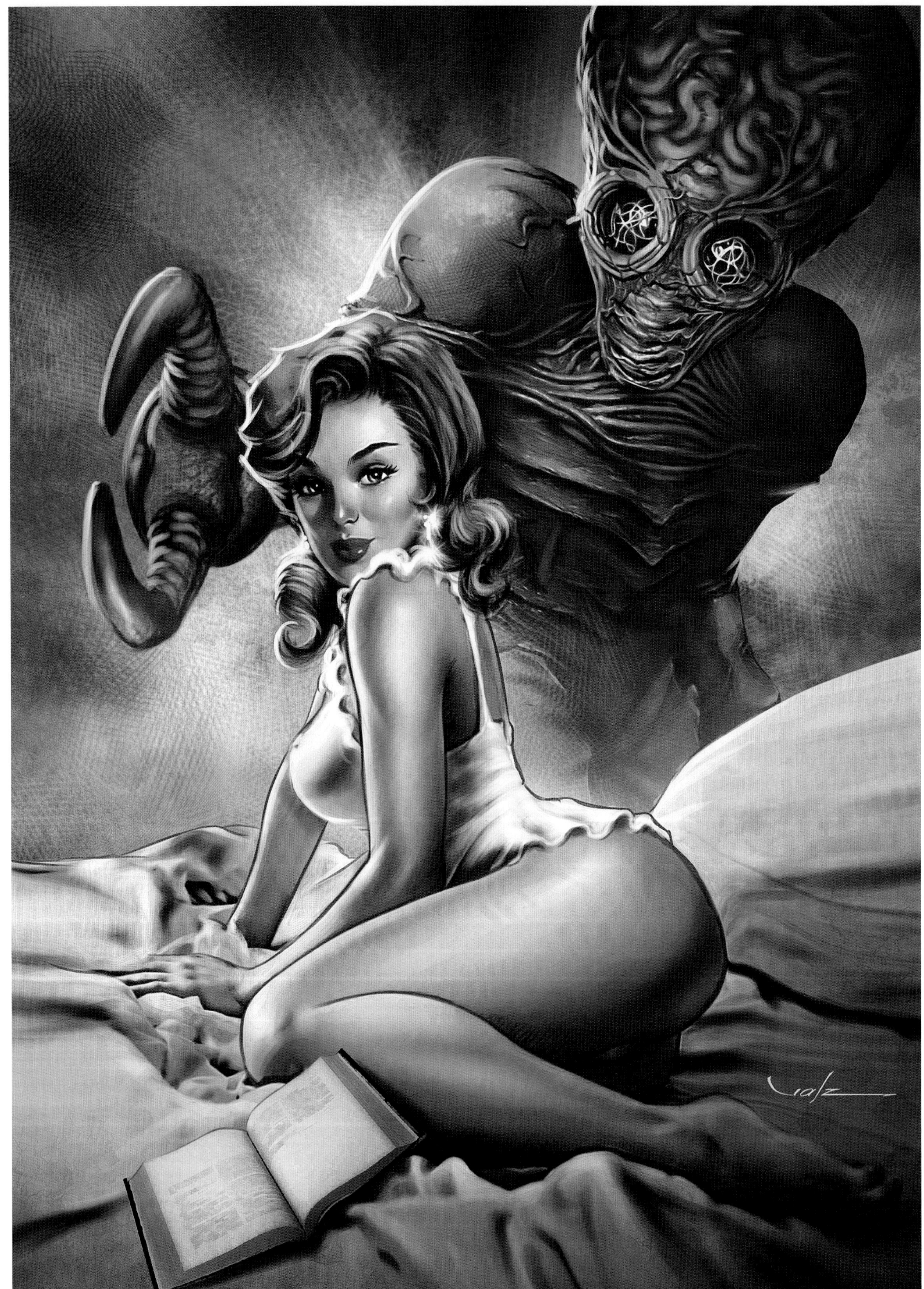

The Visitor

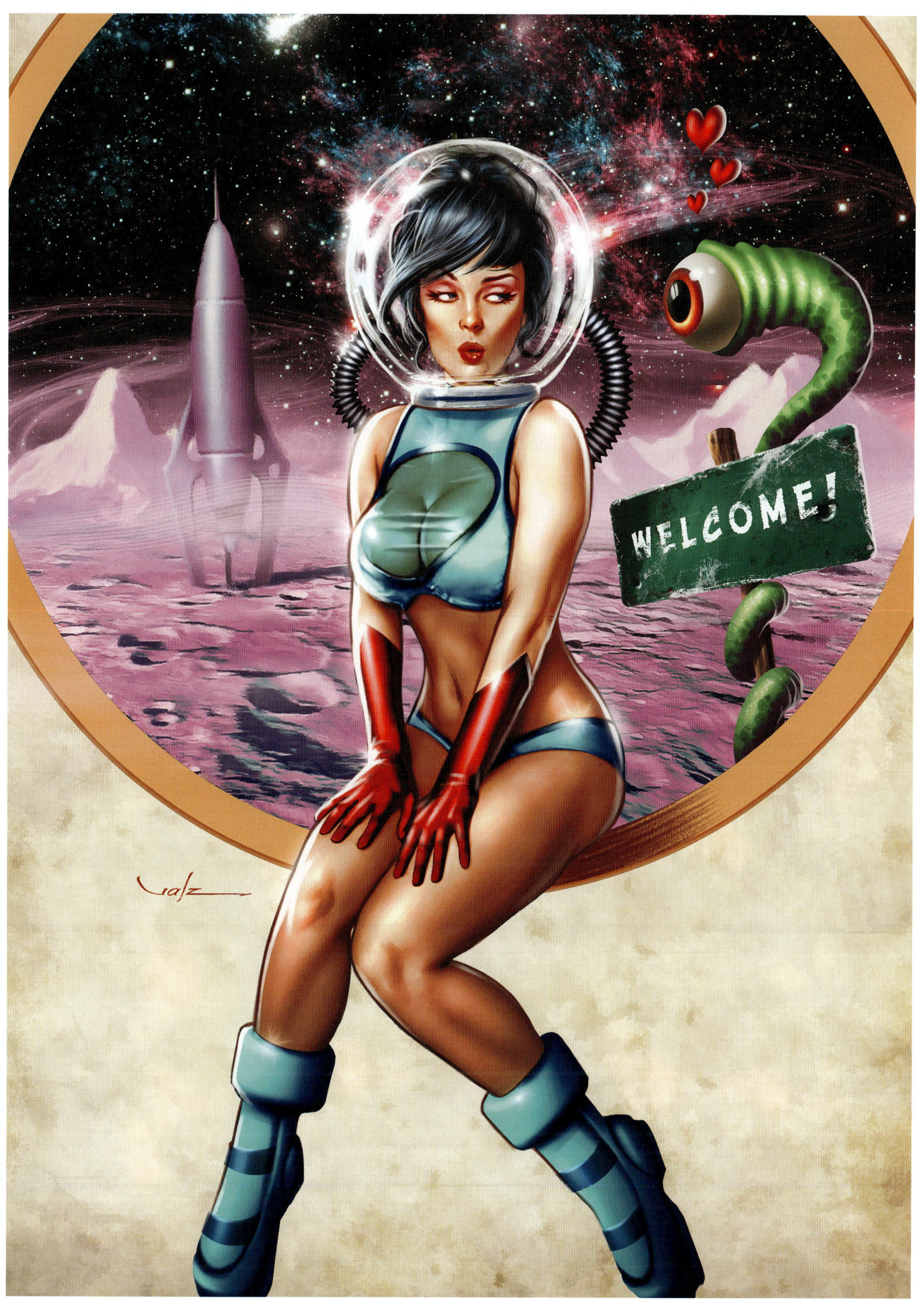

Love At First Sight

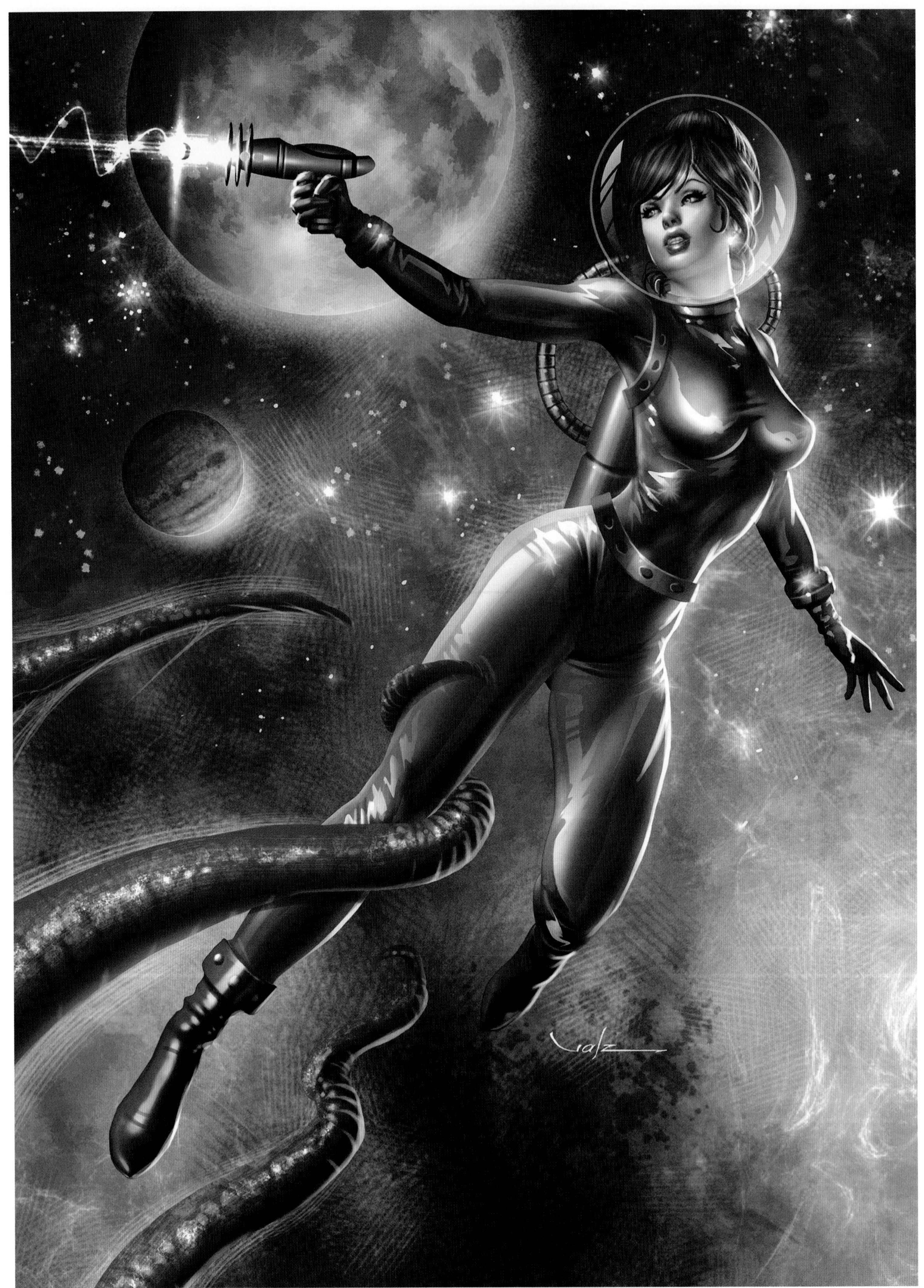

Space Vixen

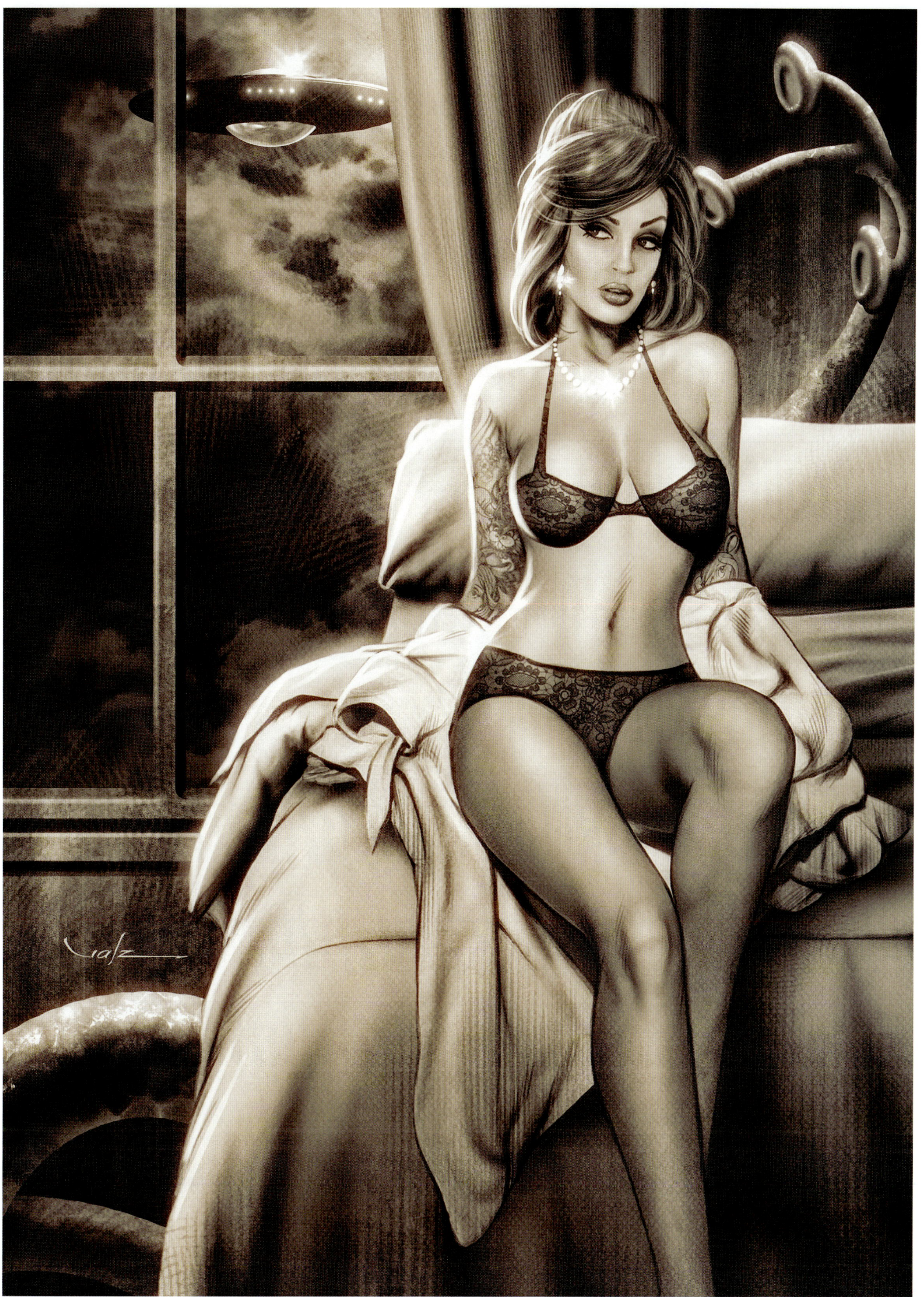

Waiting For Bedtime

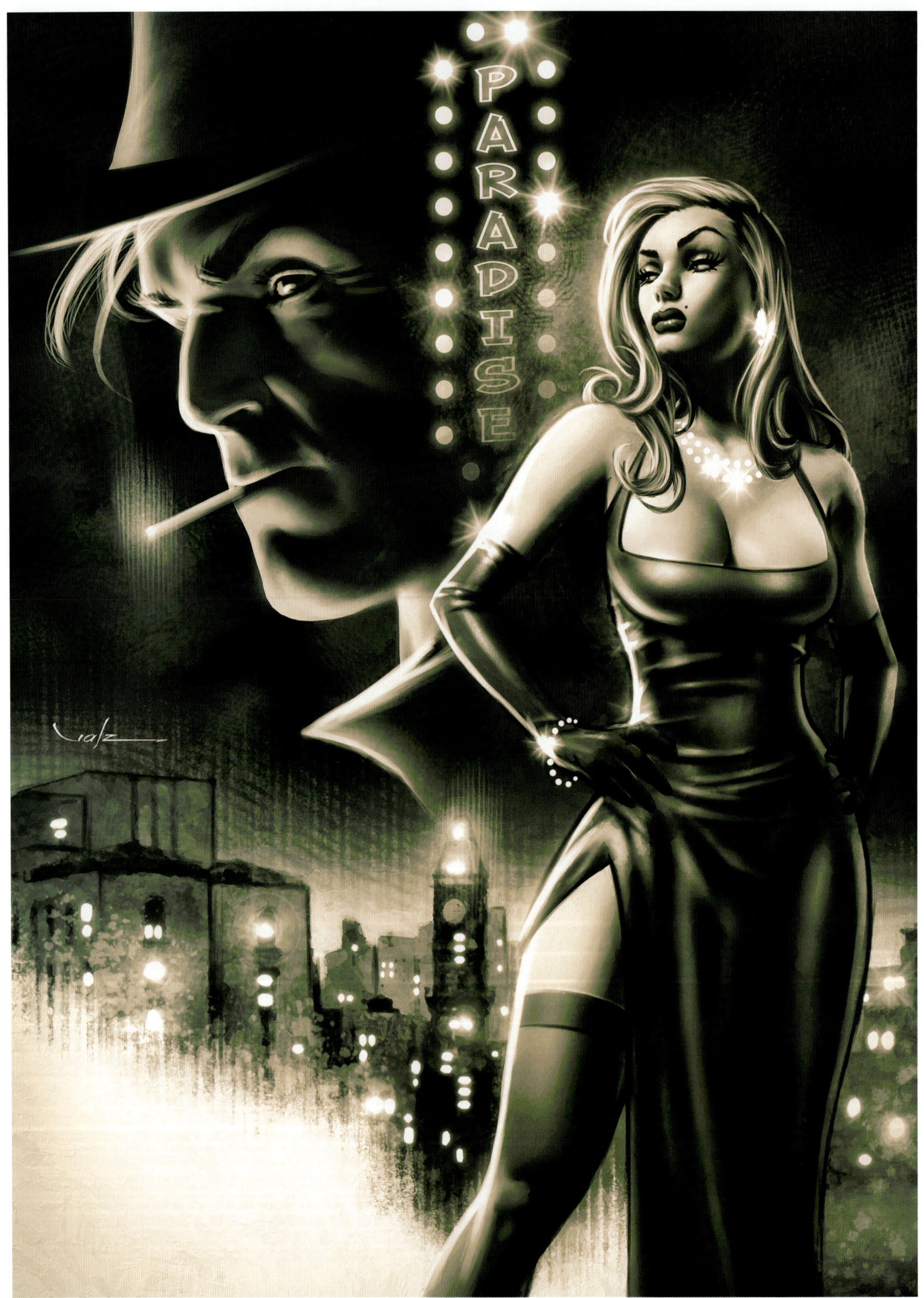

Sleep Forever

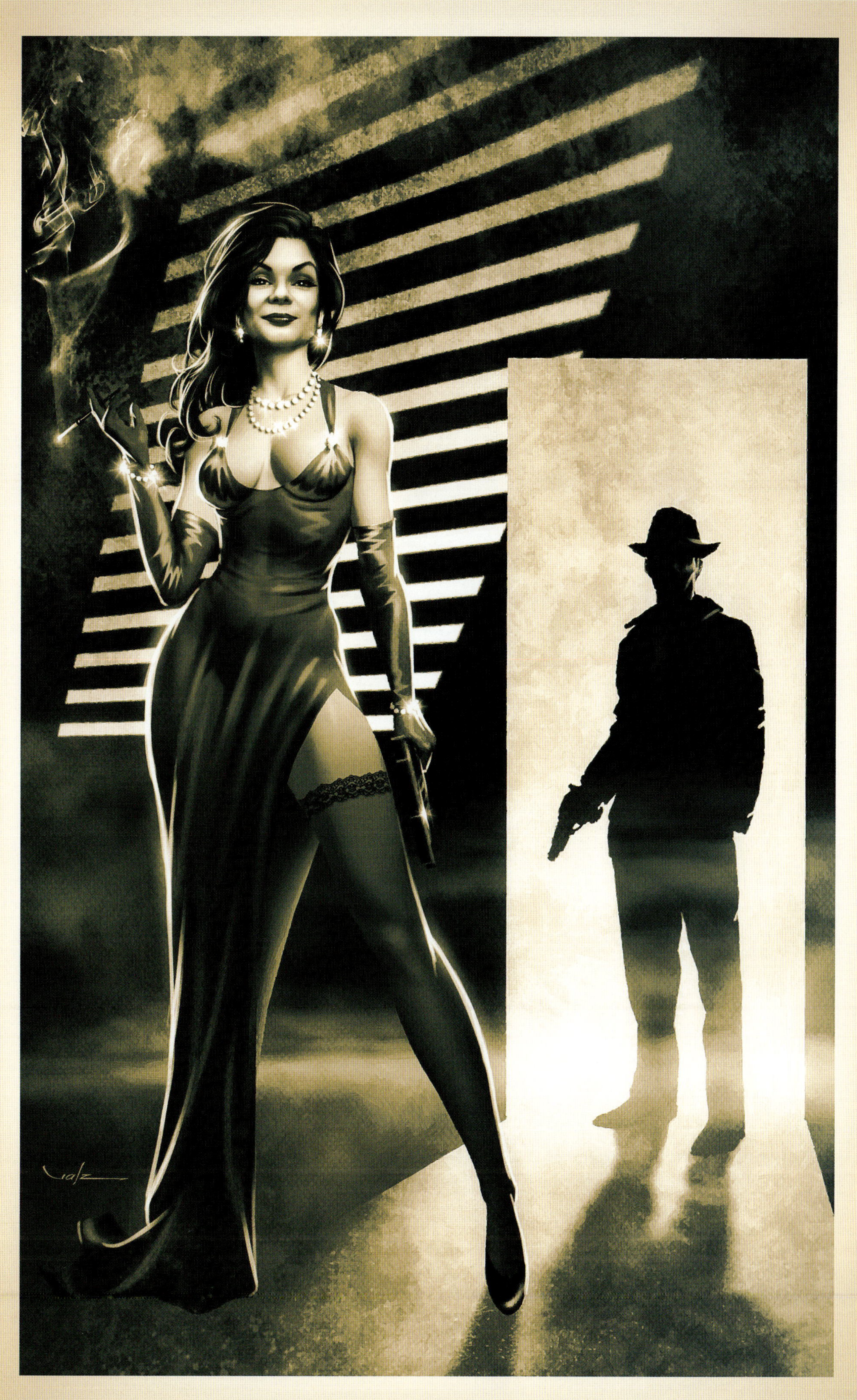

Miami Confidential

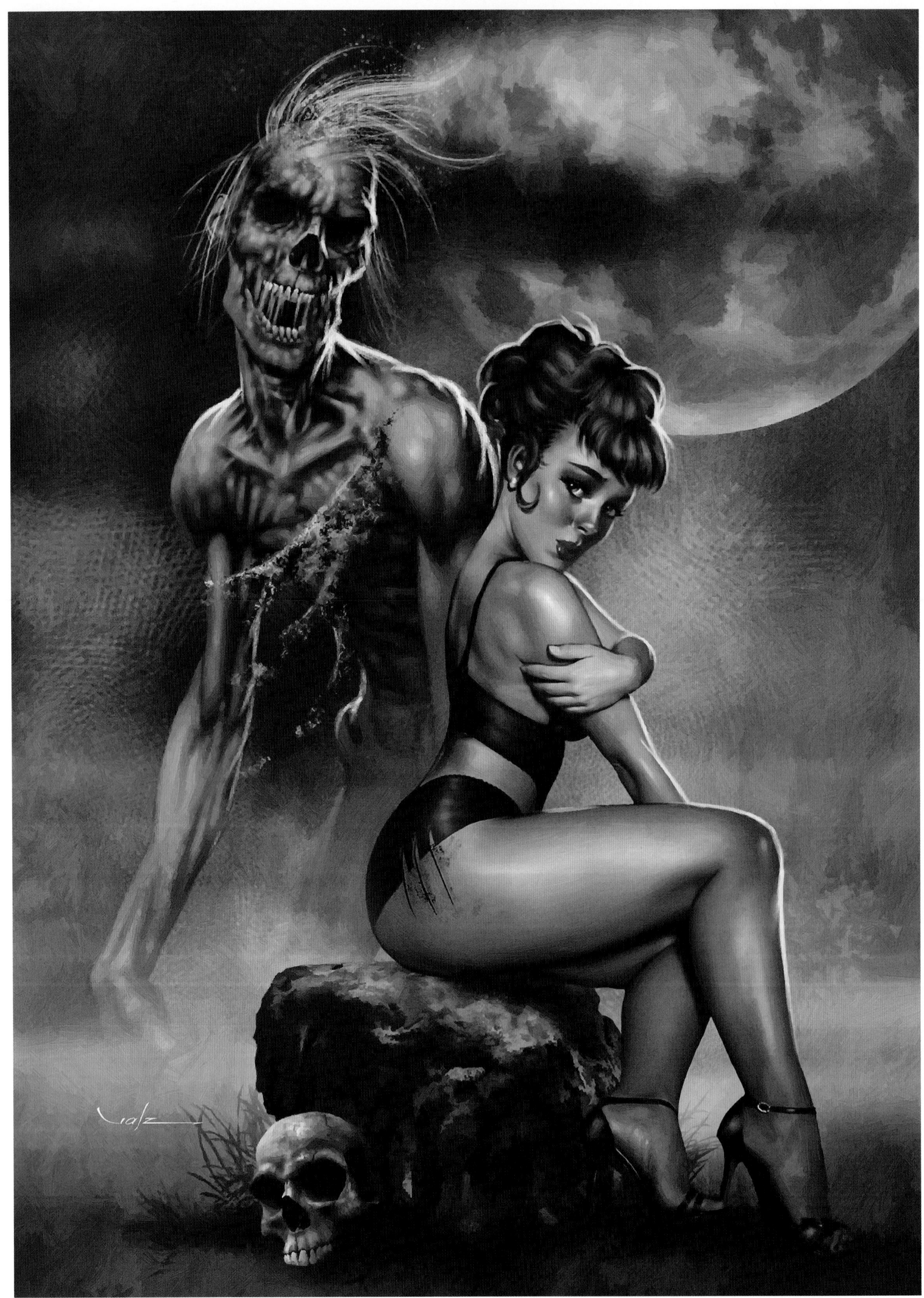

Beware The Fog

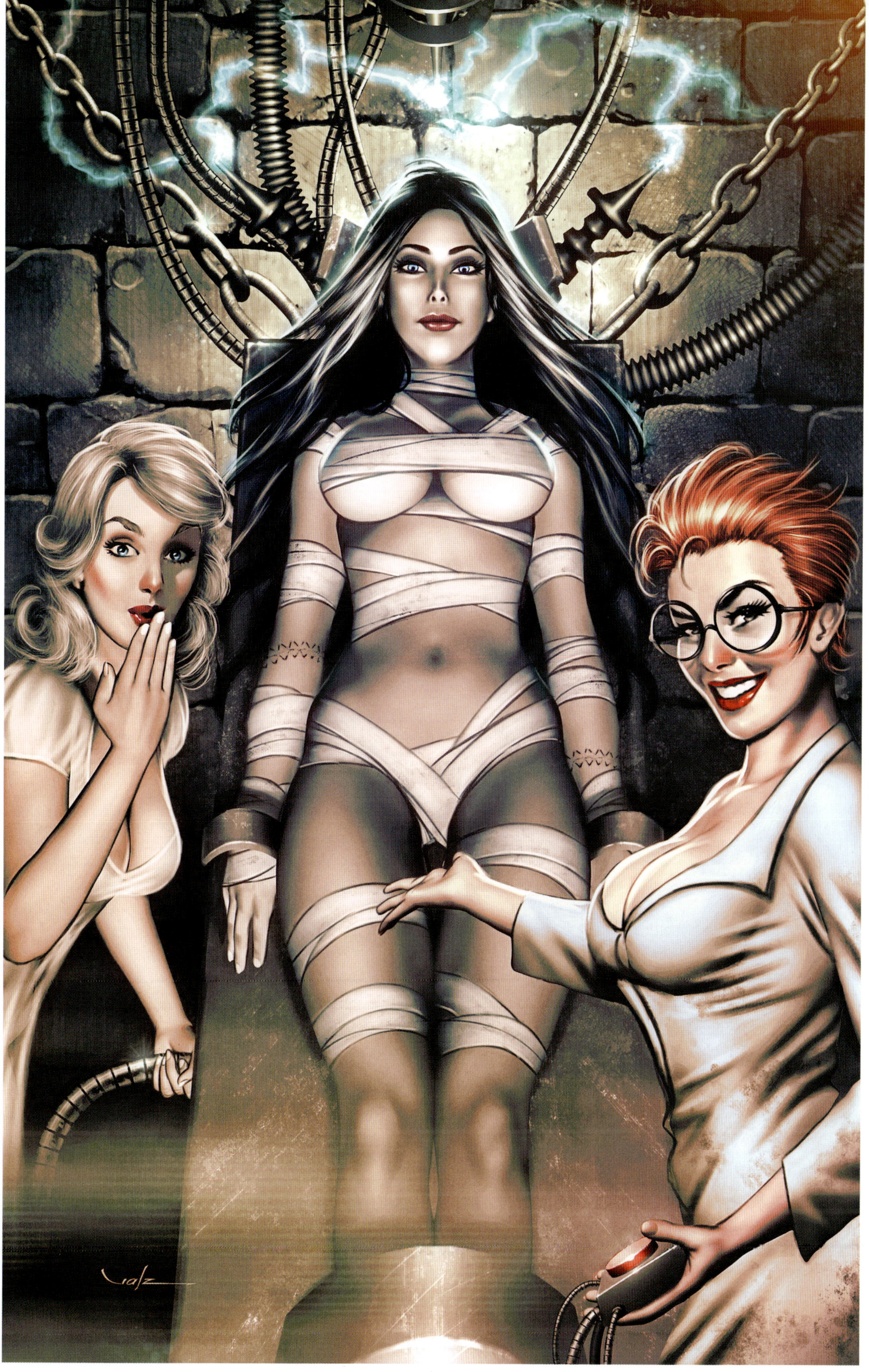

New Bride

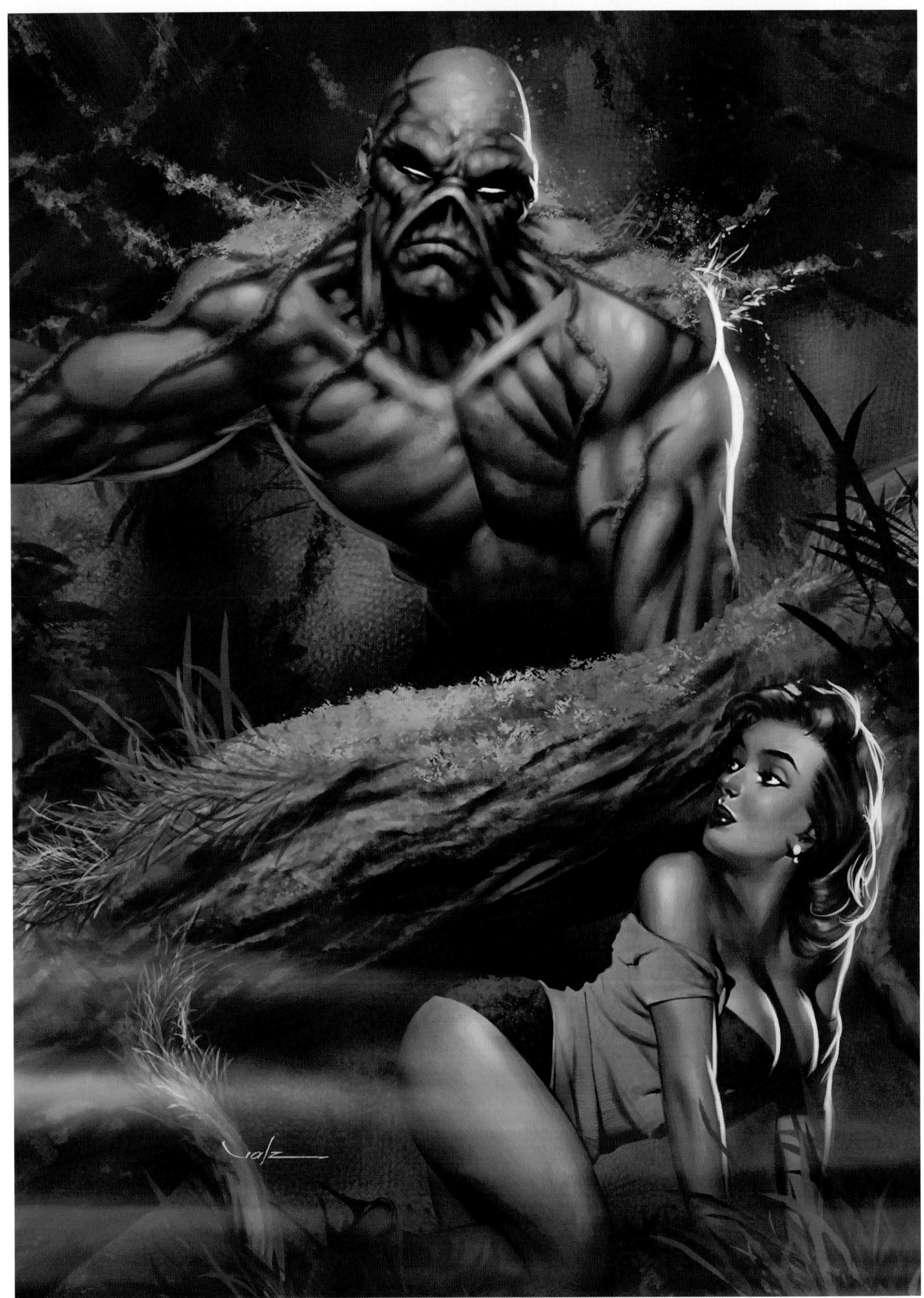

LOOK BEHIND YOU

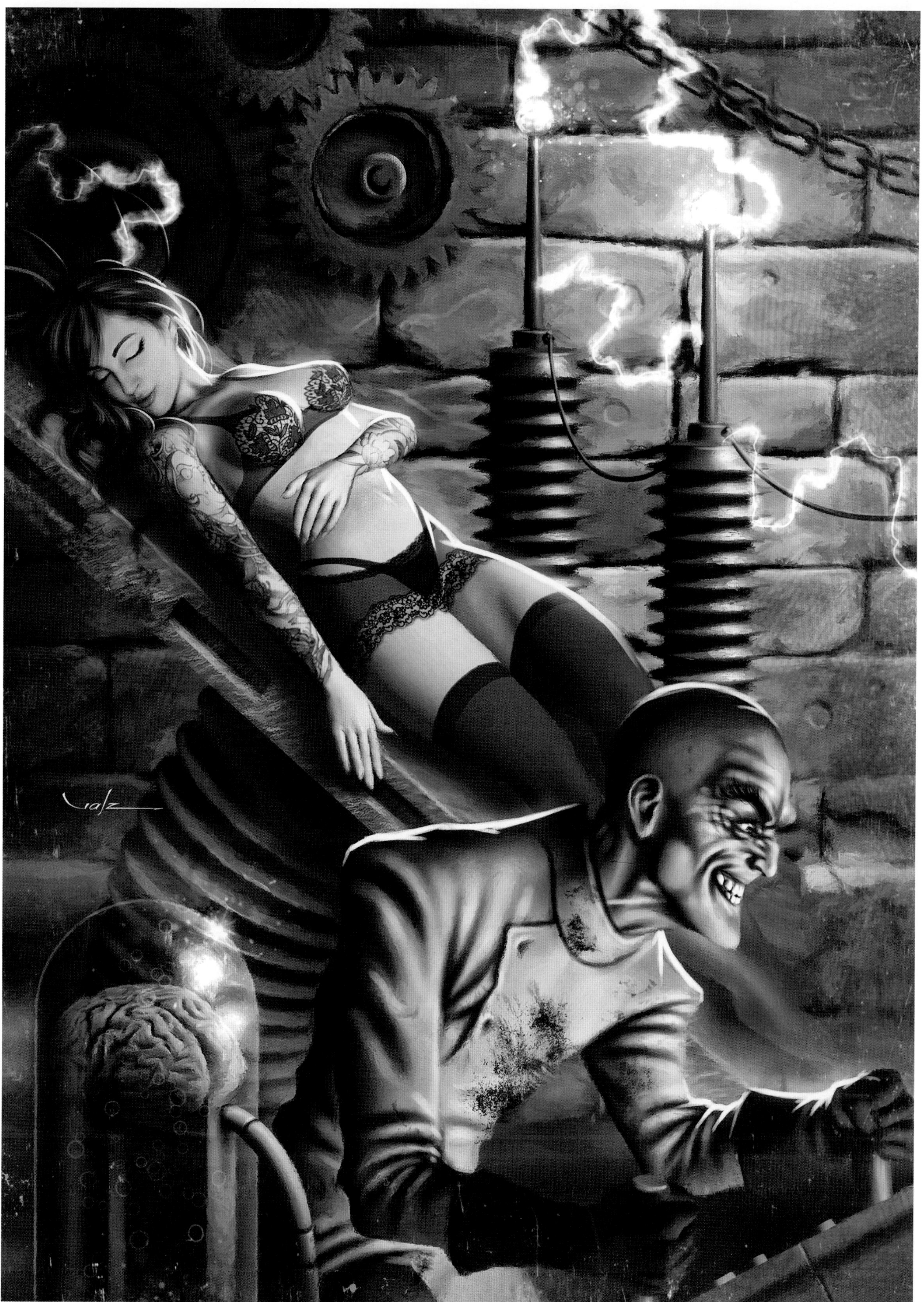

It's Alive!

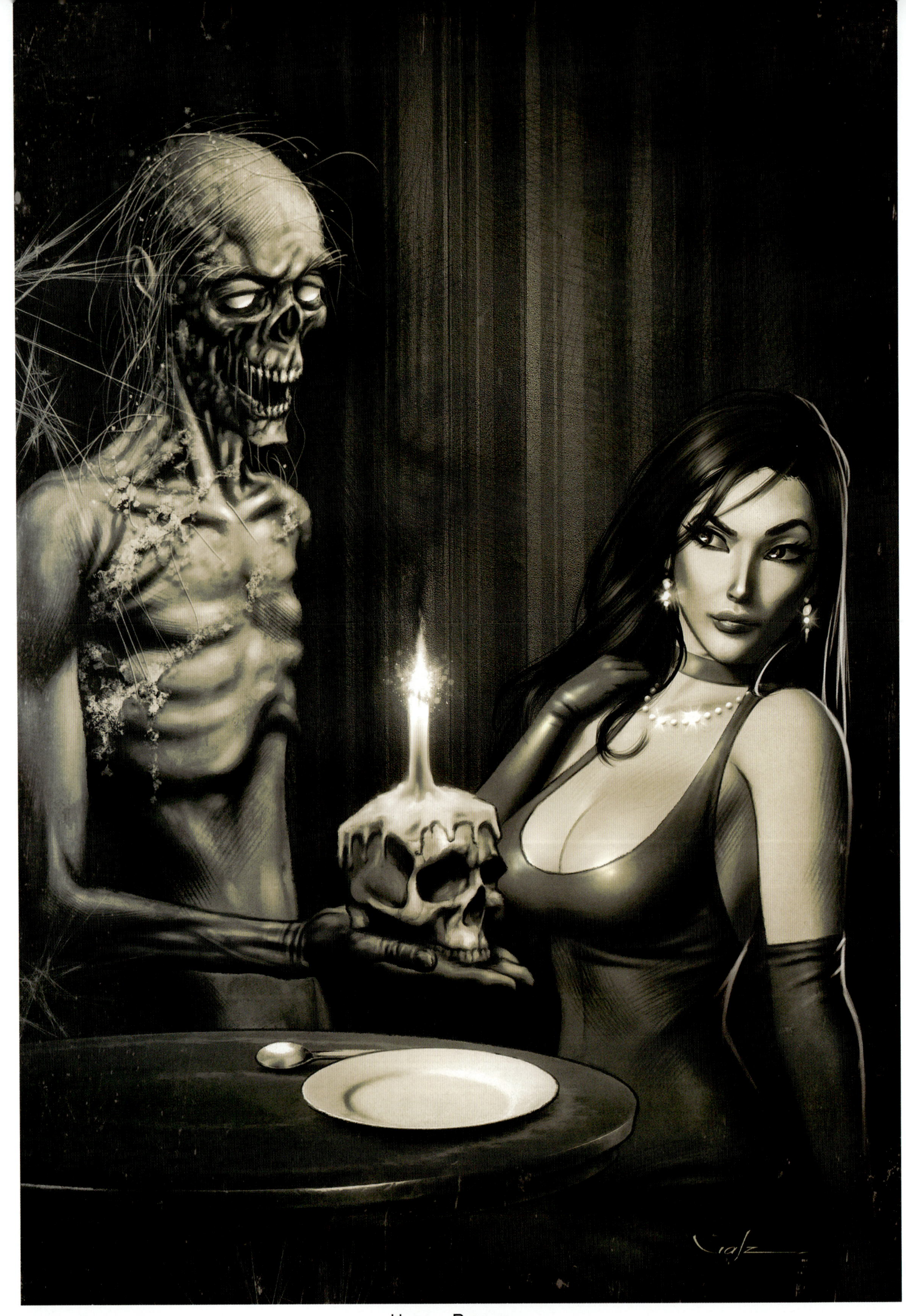

HAPPY BIRTHDAY

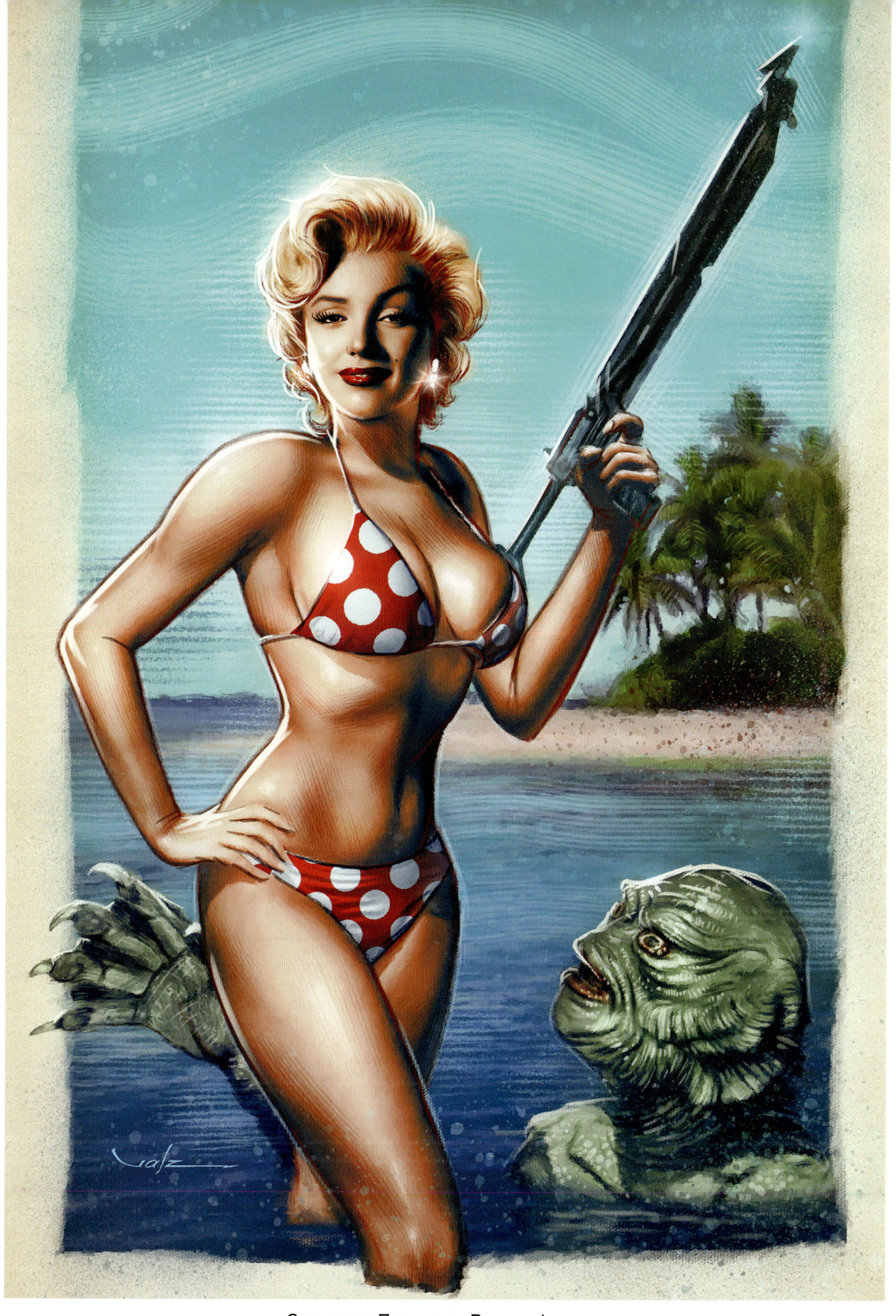

Creature From the Blonde Lagoon

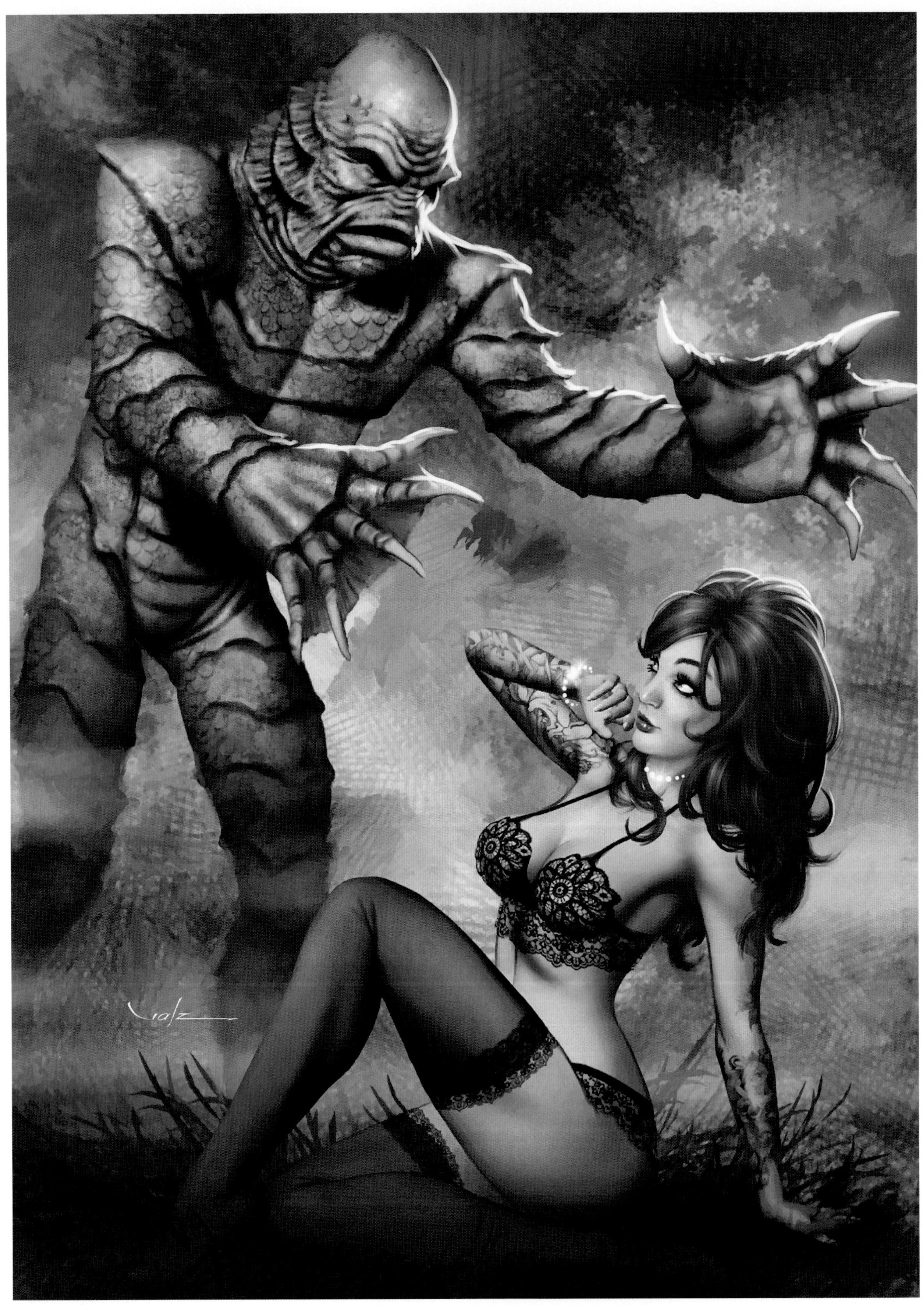

OUT OF HIS LEAGUE

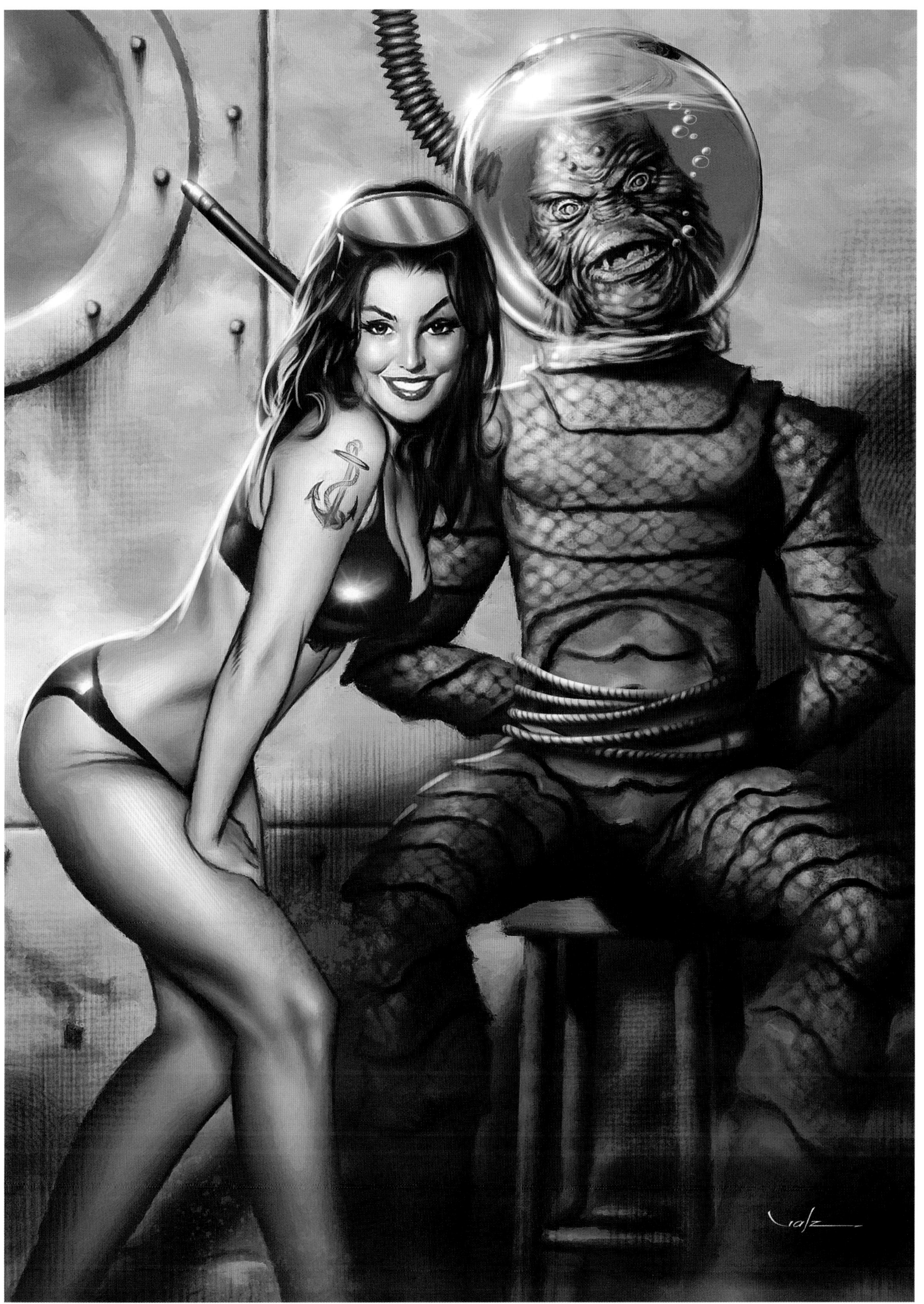

CREATURE EXPOSED

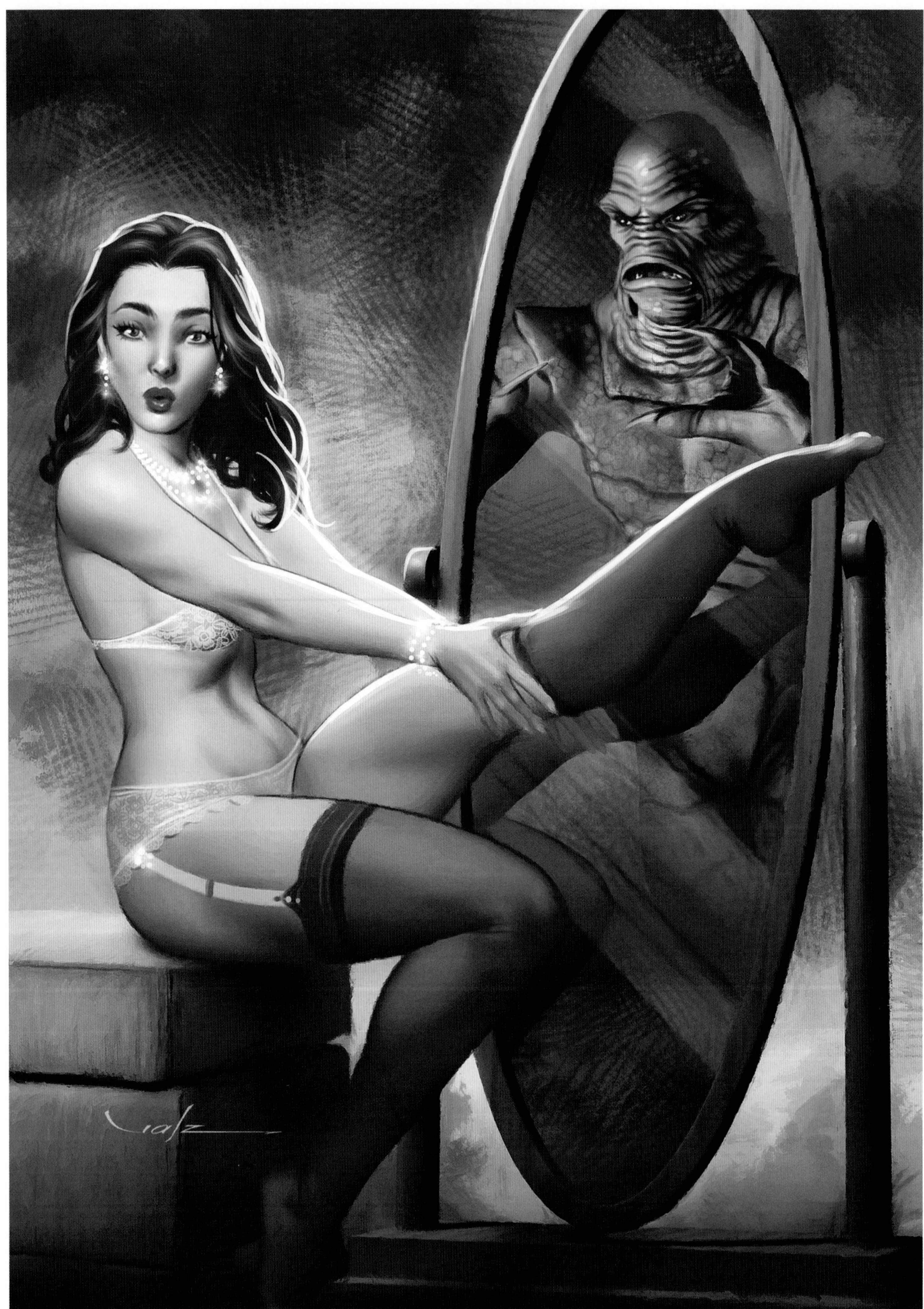

Don't Look

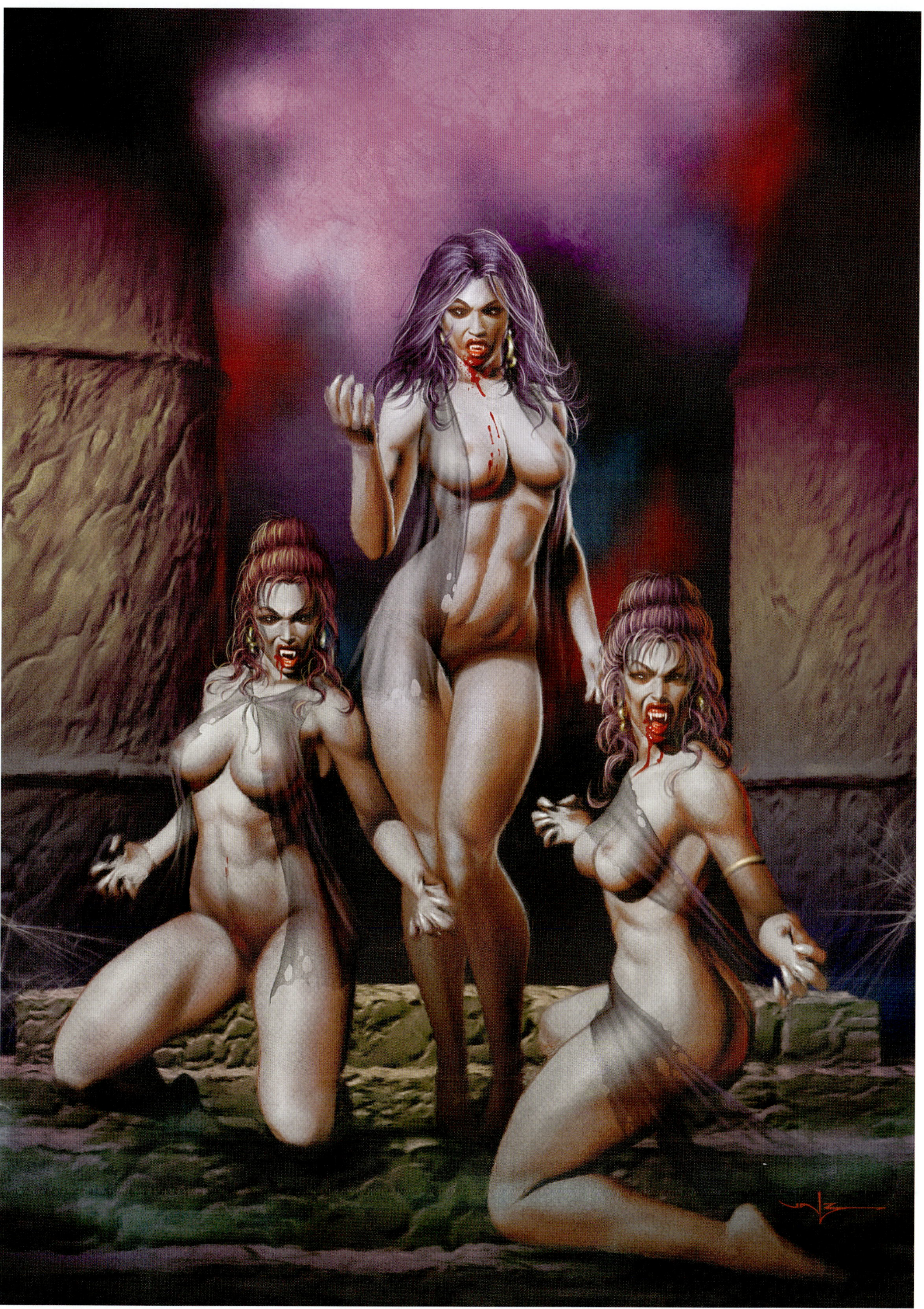

Lovers From Hell

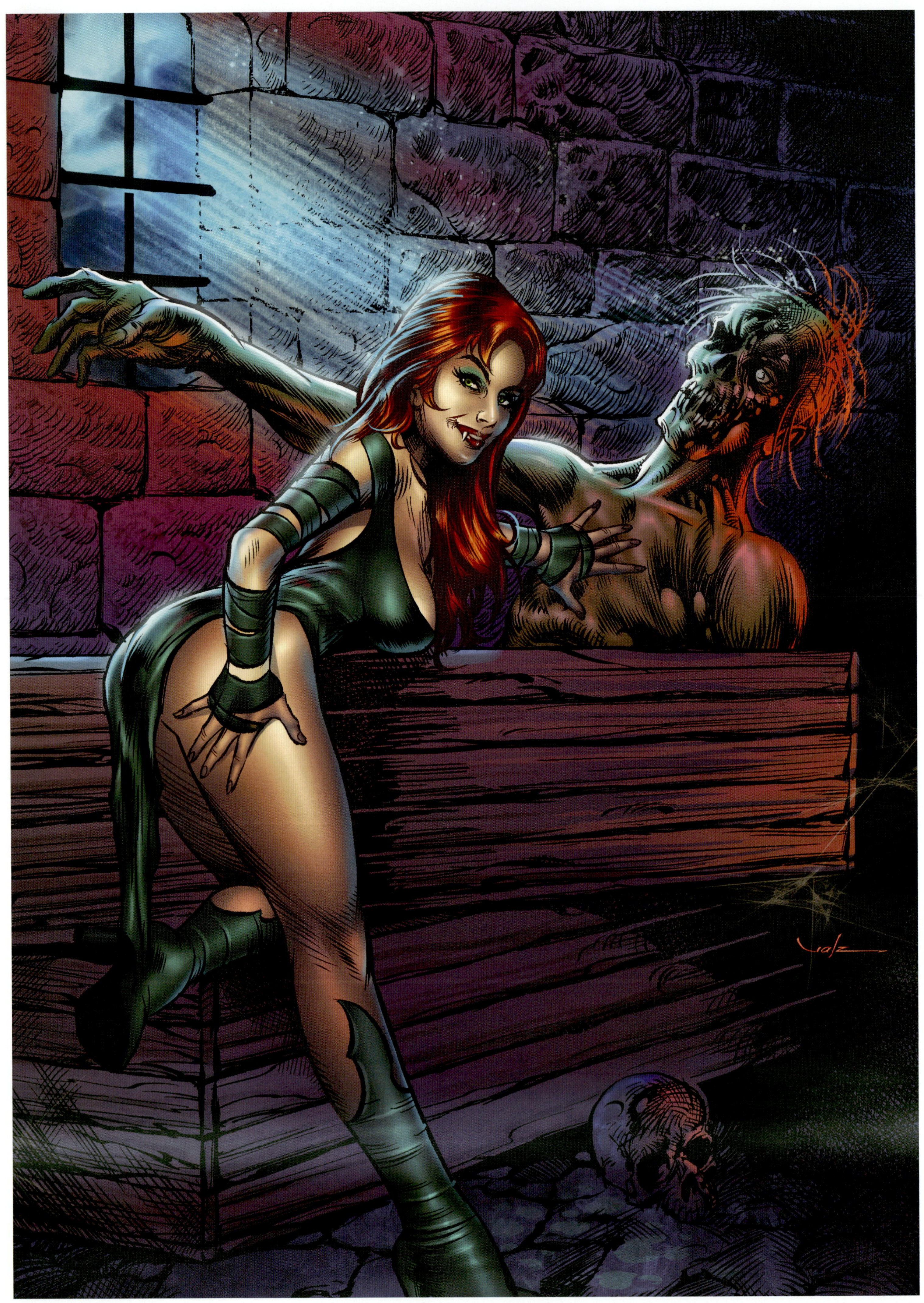

Awaken The Corpse

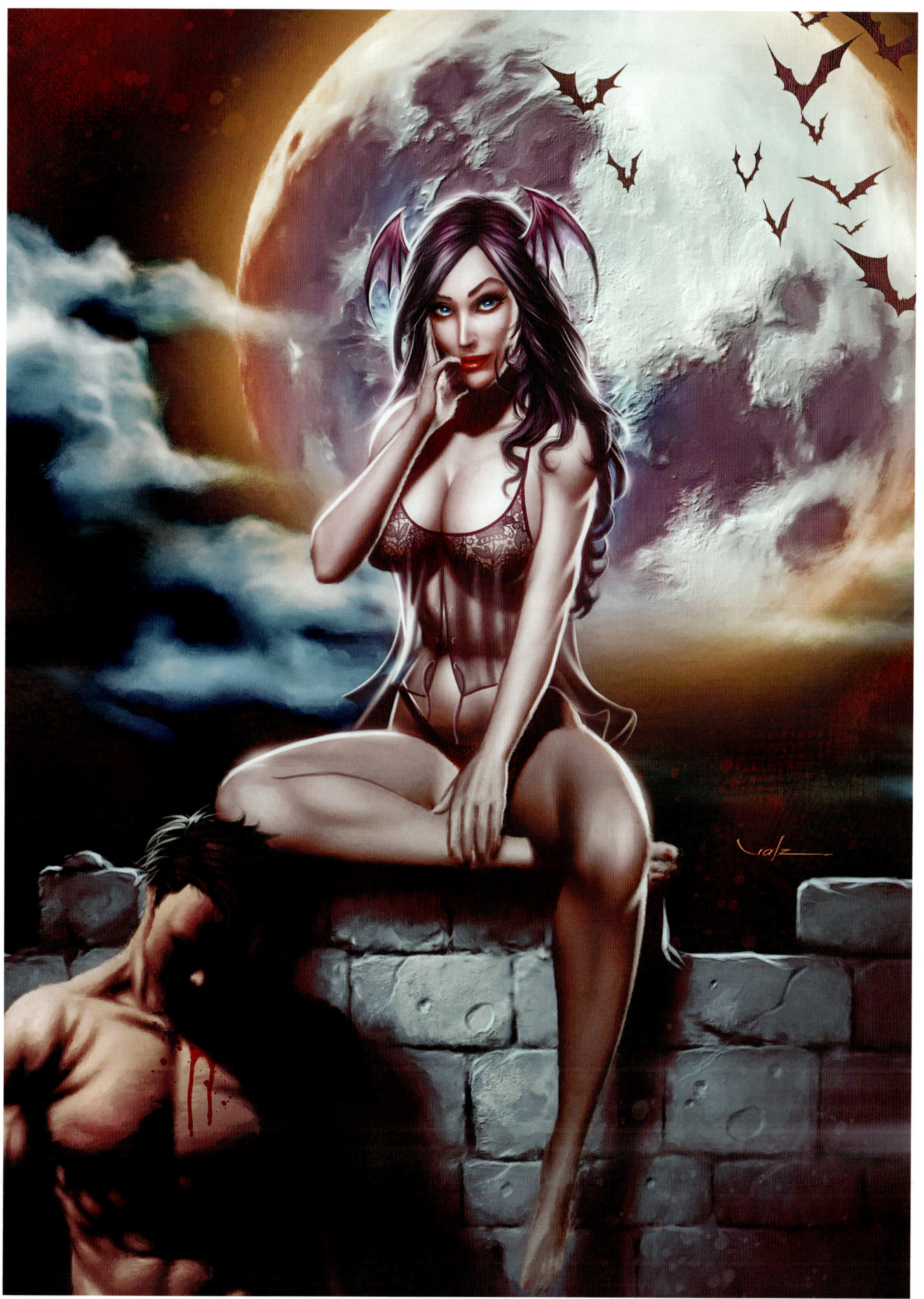

Vampire's Last Kiss

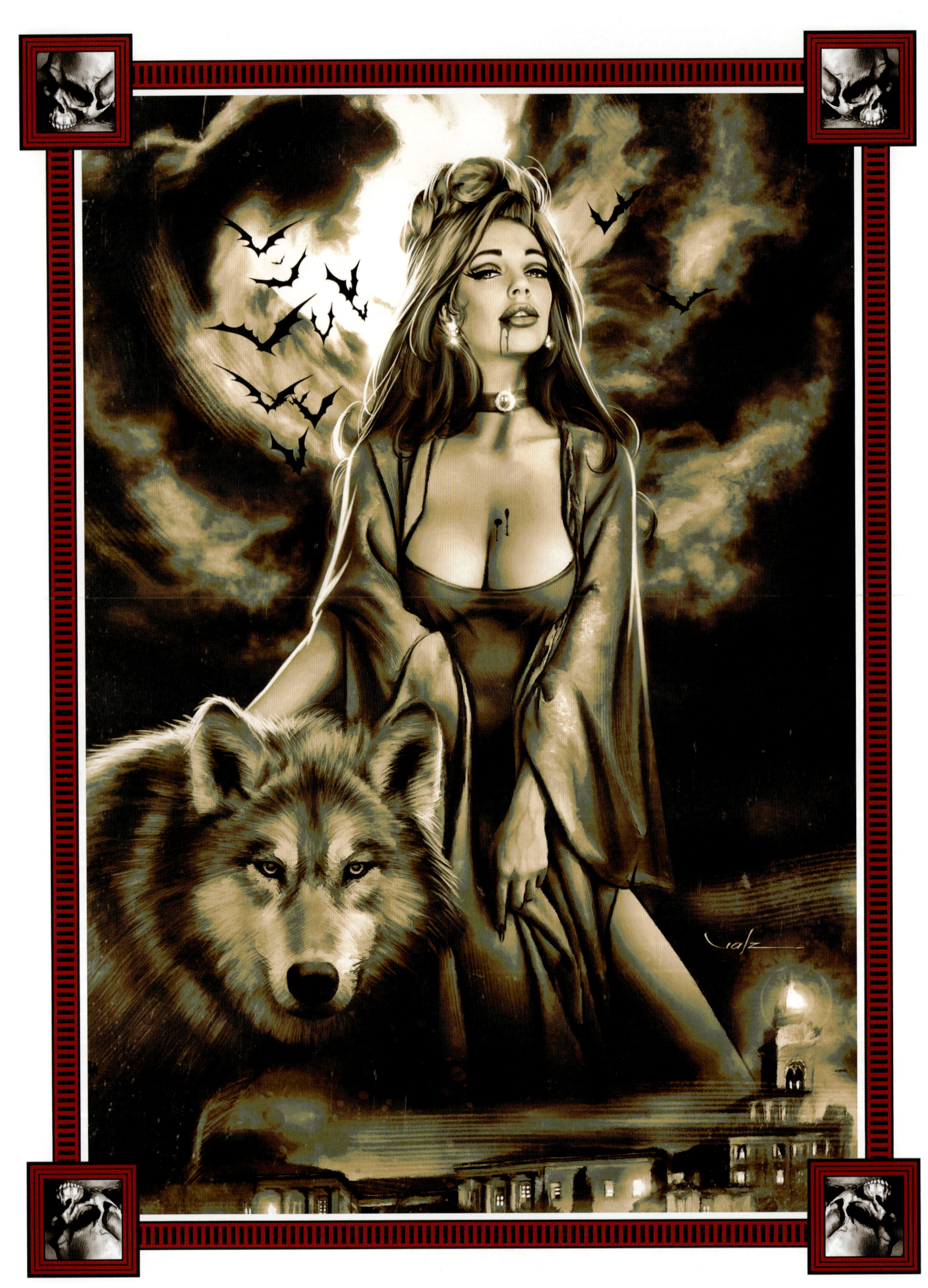

VAMPIRE QUEEN

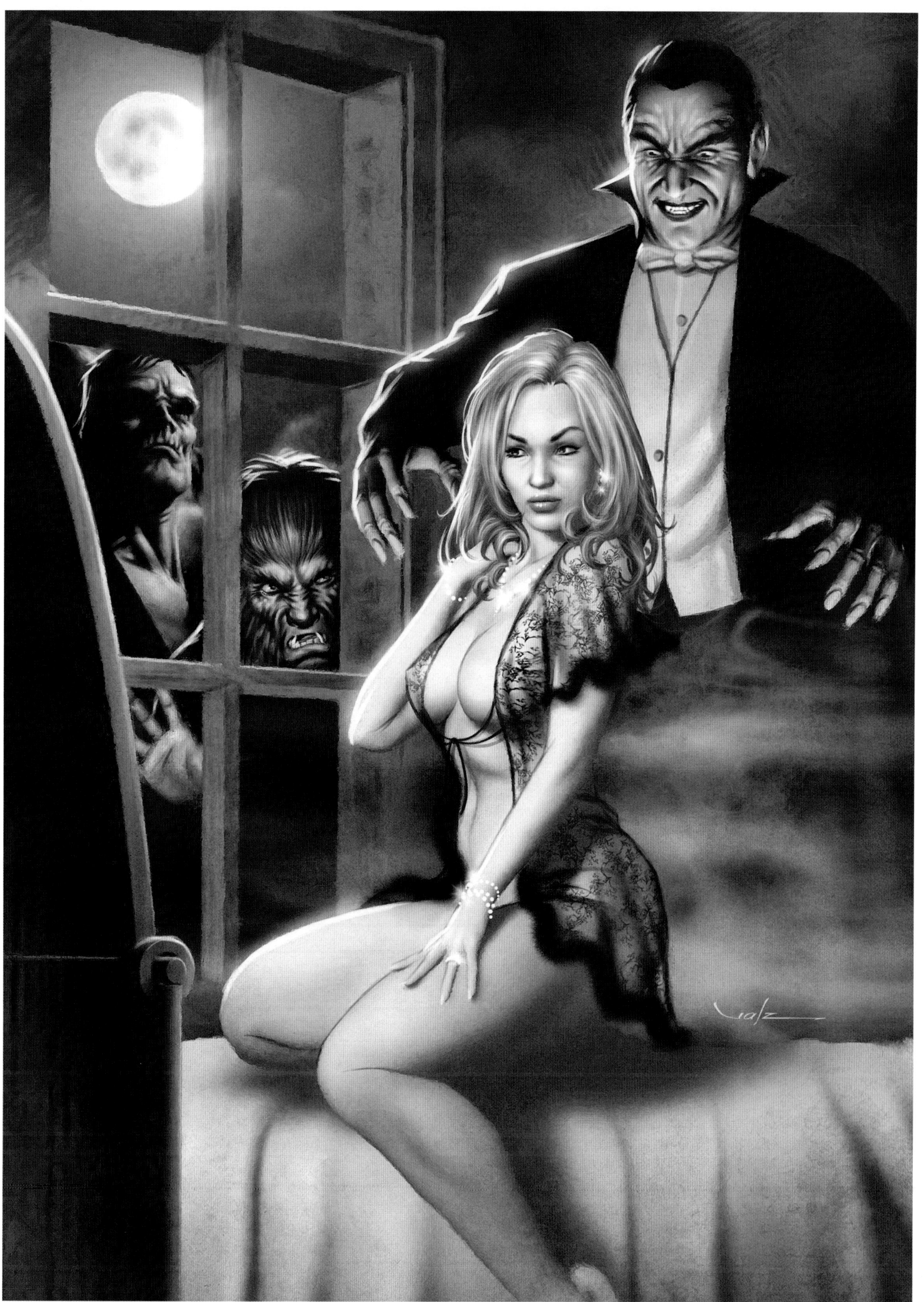

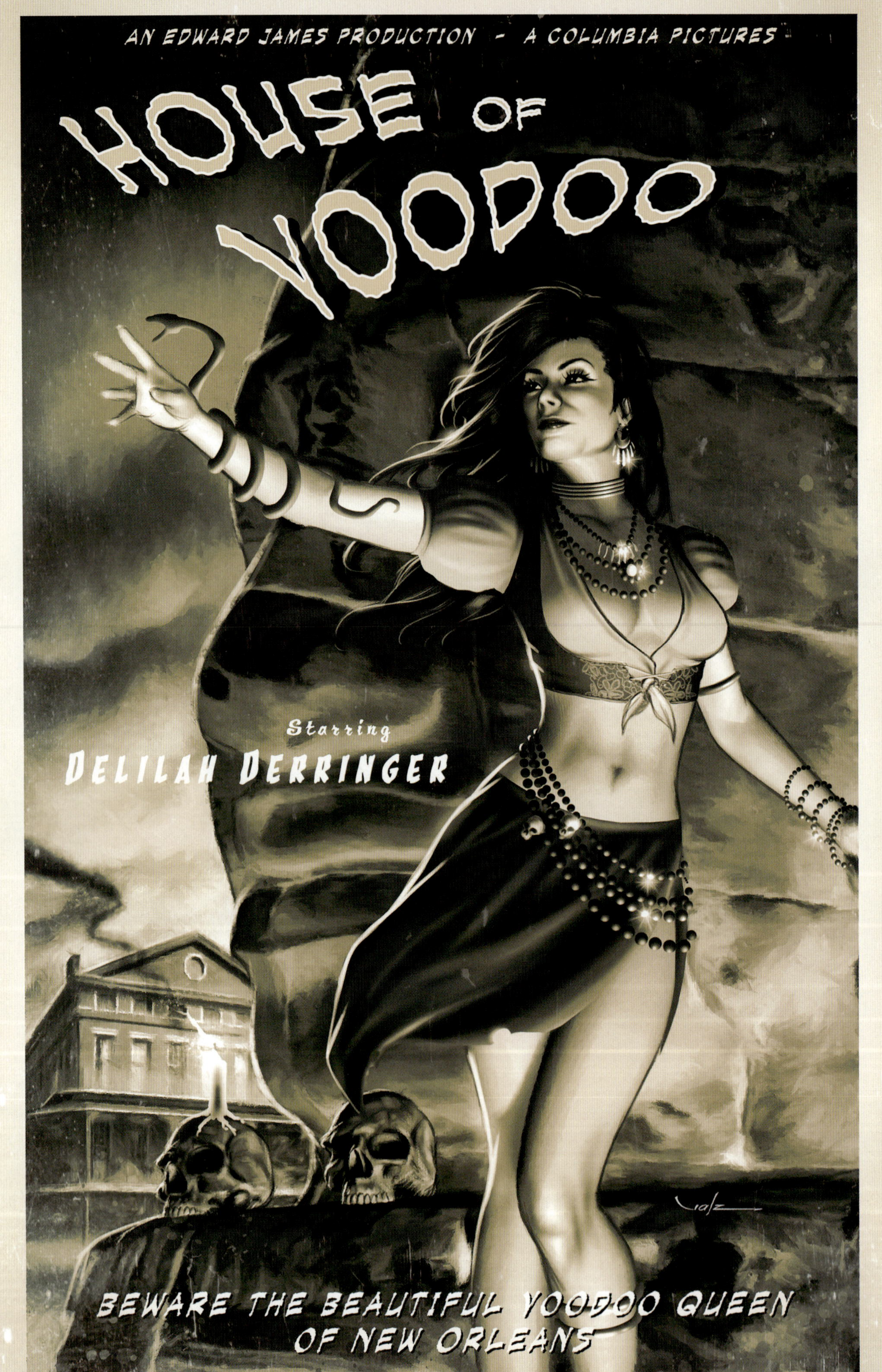

Voodoo Queen

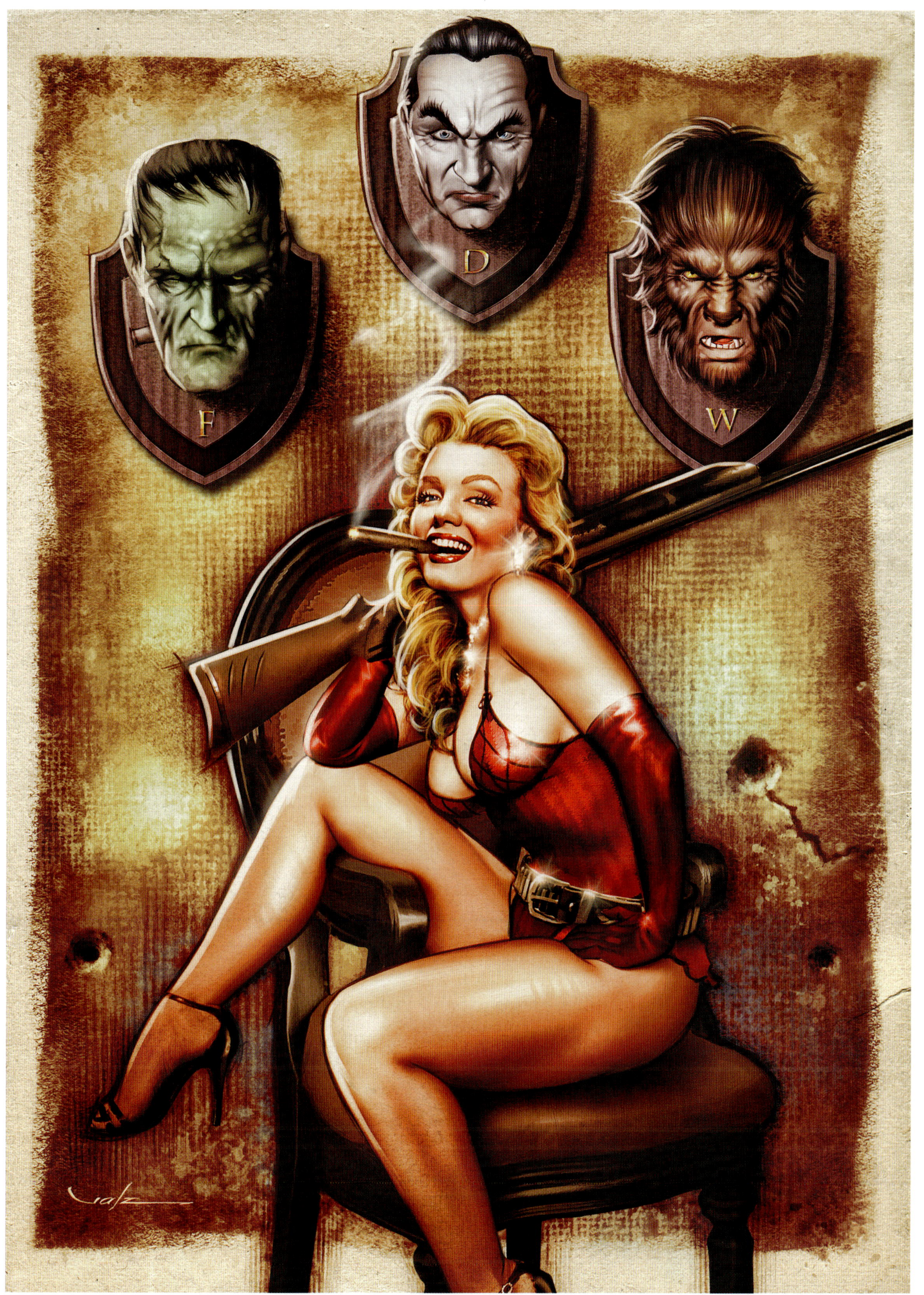

THE HUNTRESS

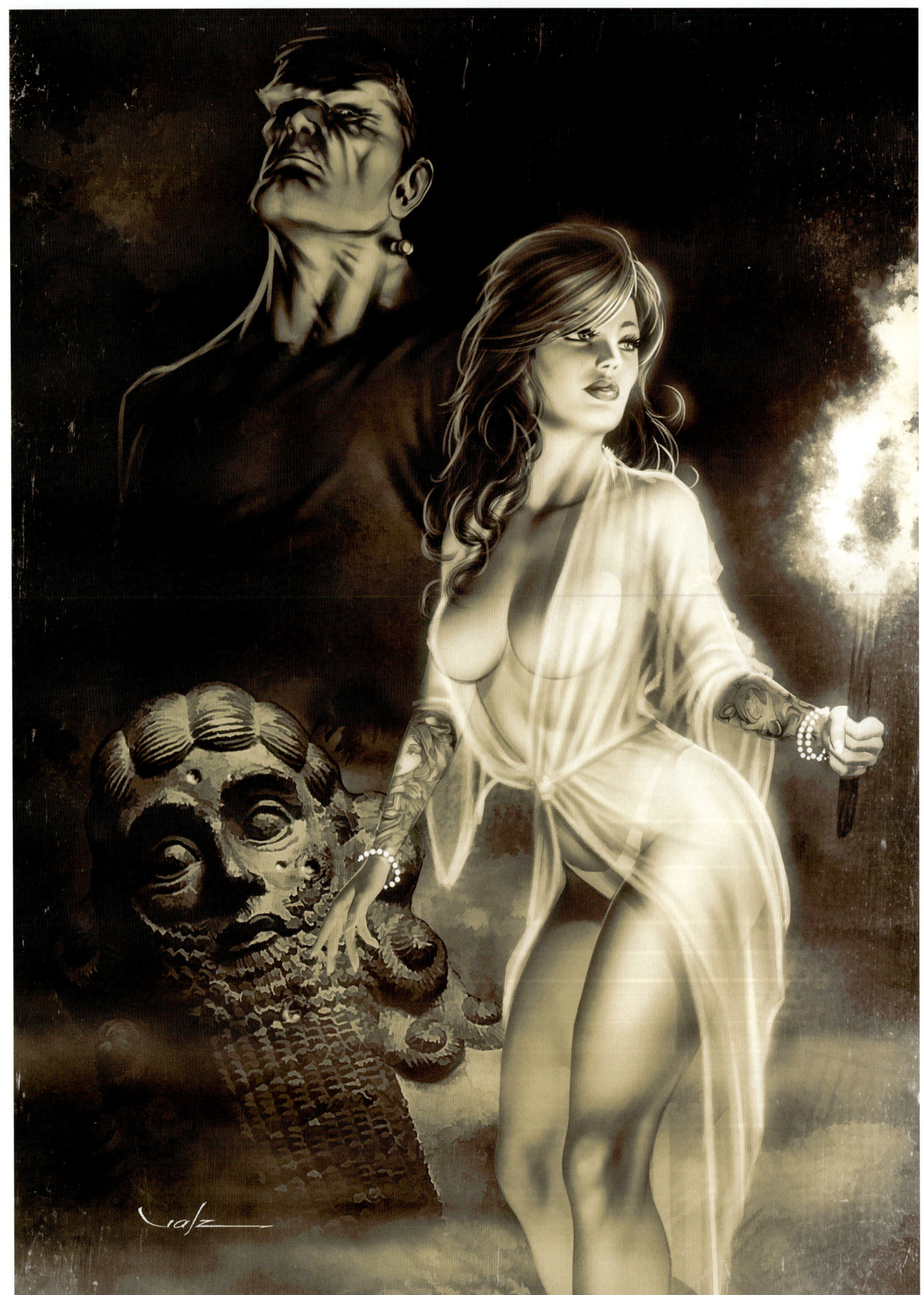

WATCH OUT

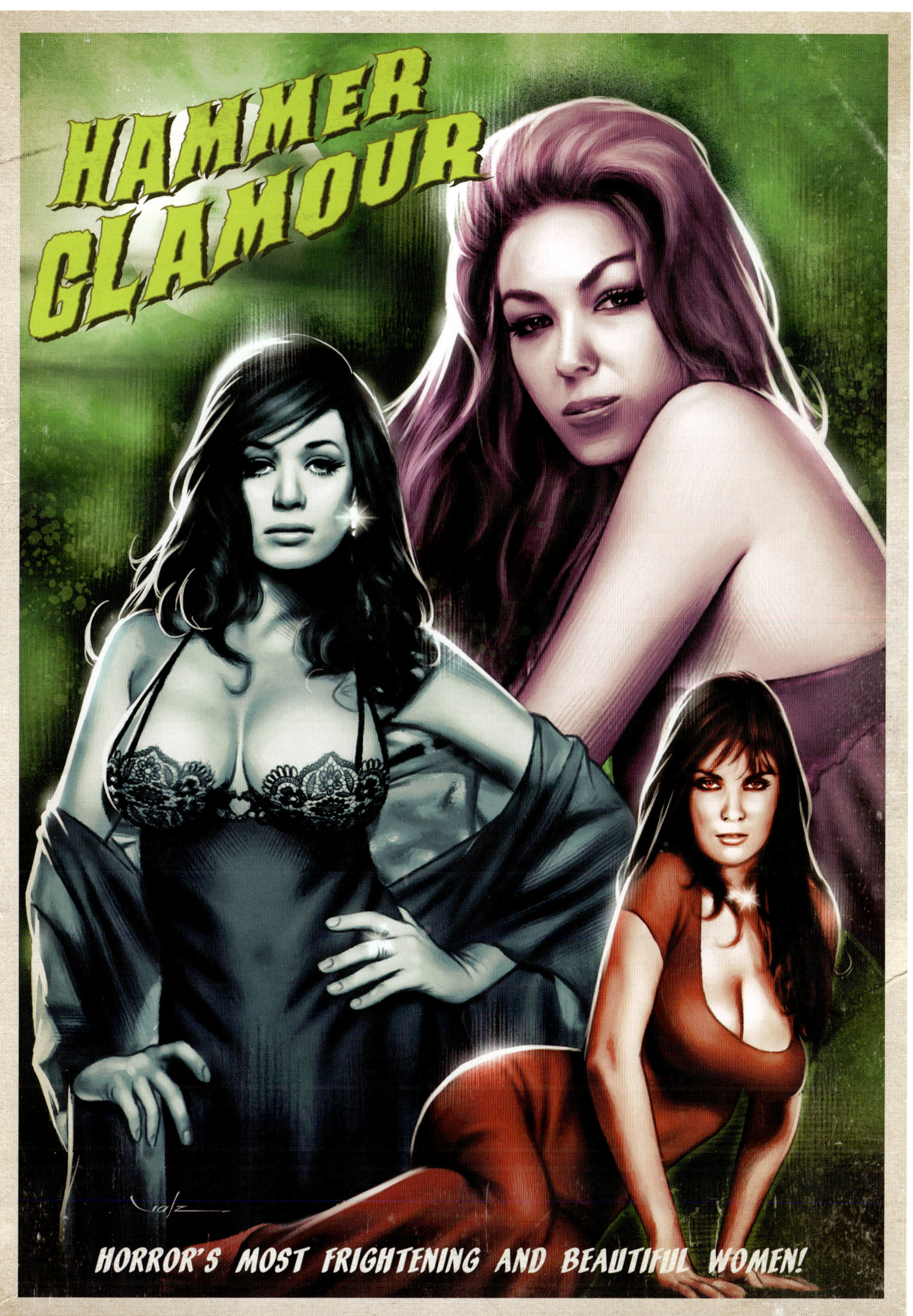

HAMMER GLAMOUR
HORROR'S MOST FRIGHTENING AND BEAUTIFUL WOMEN!

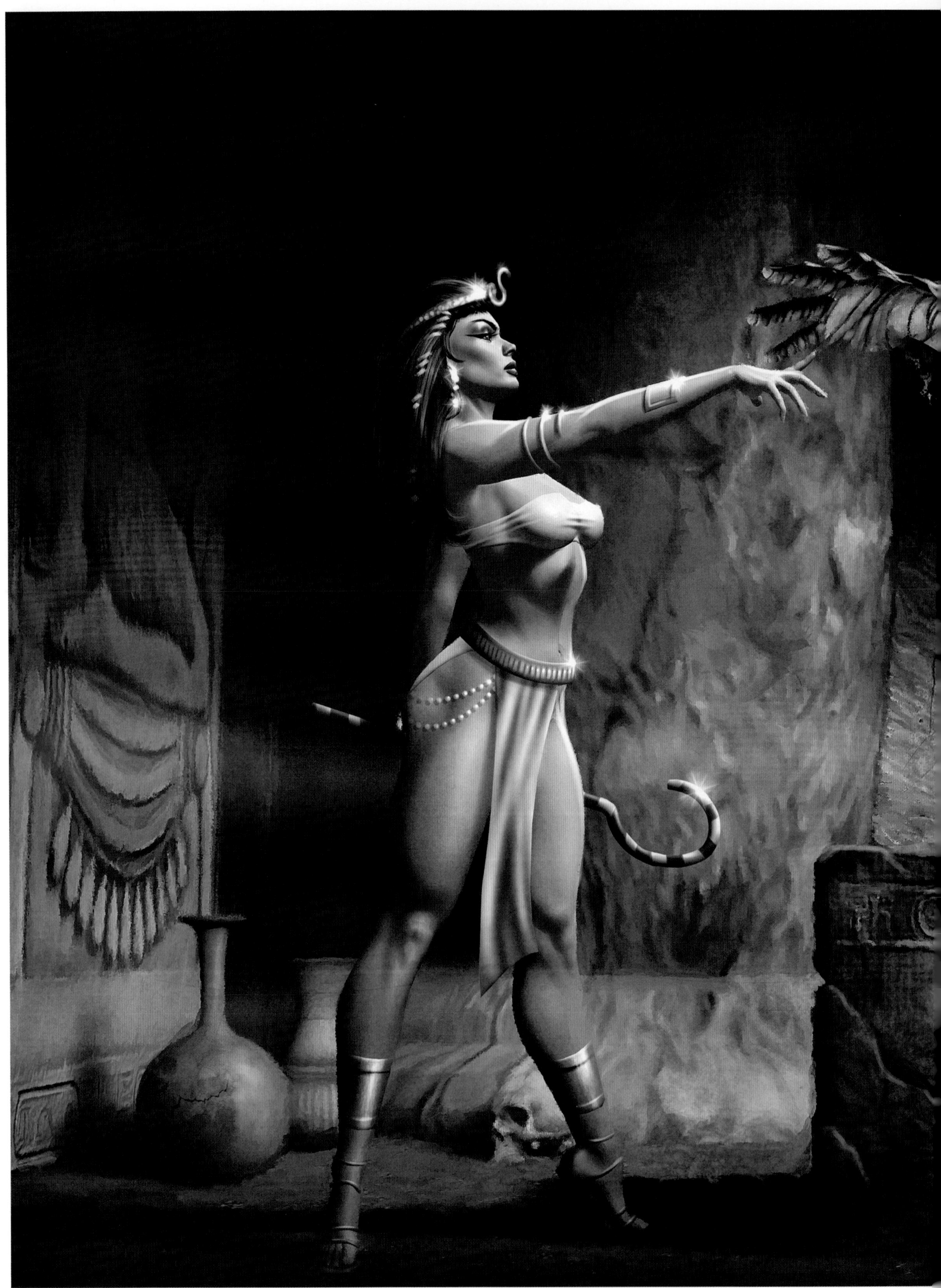

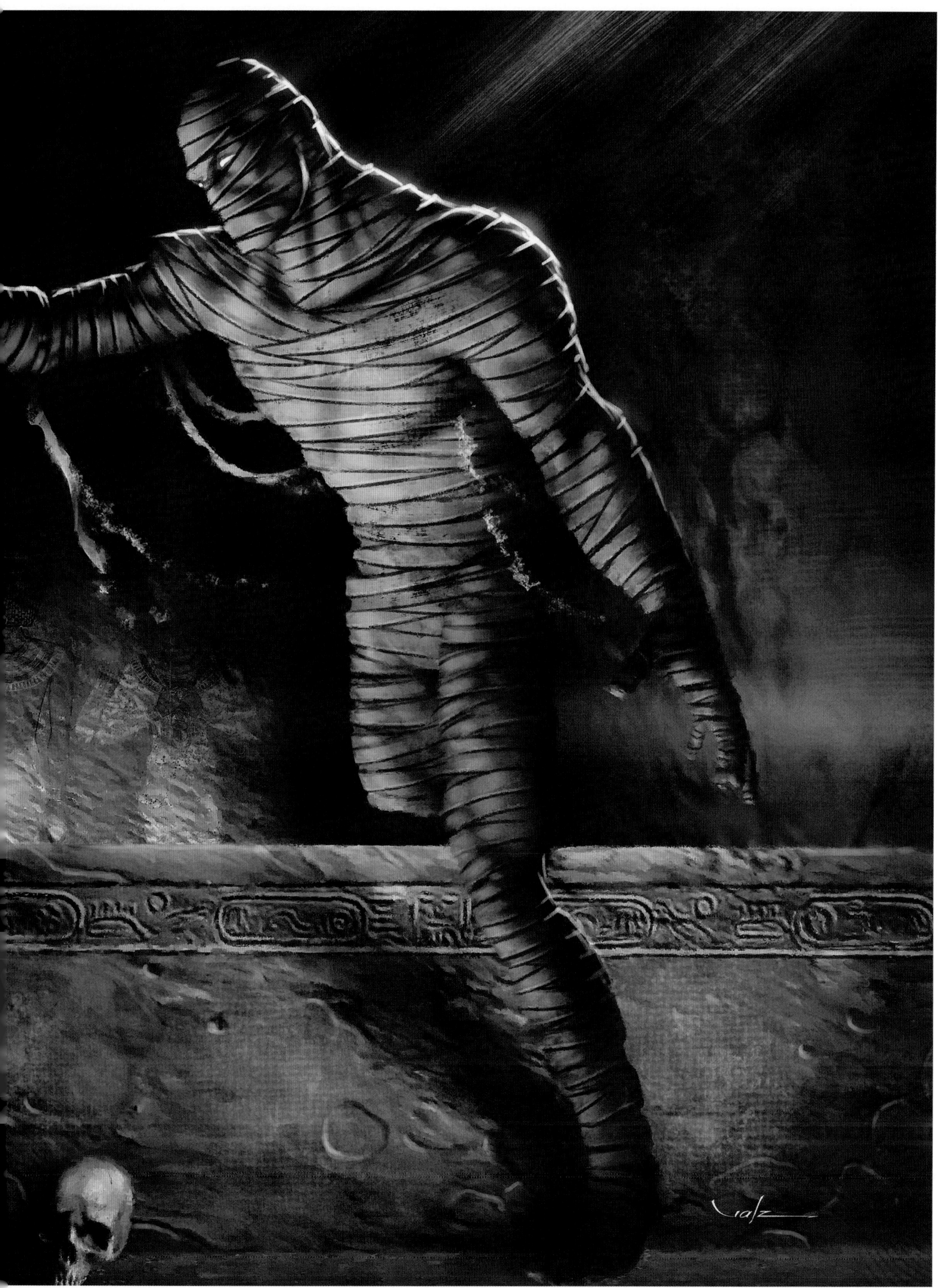

THE MUMMY

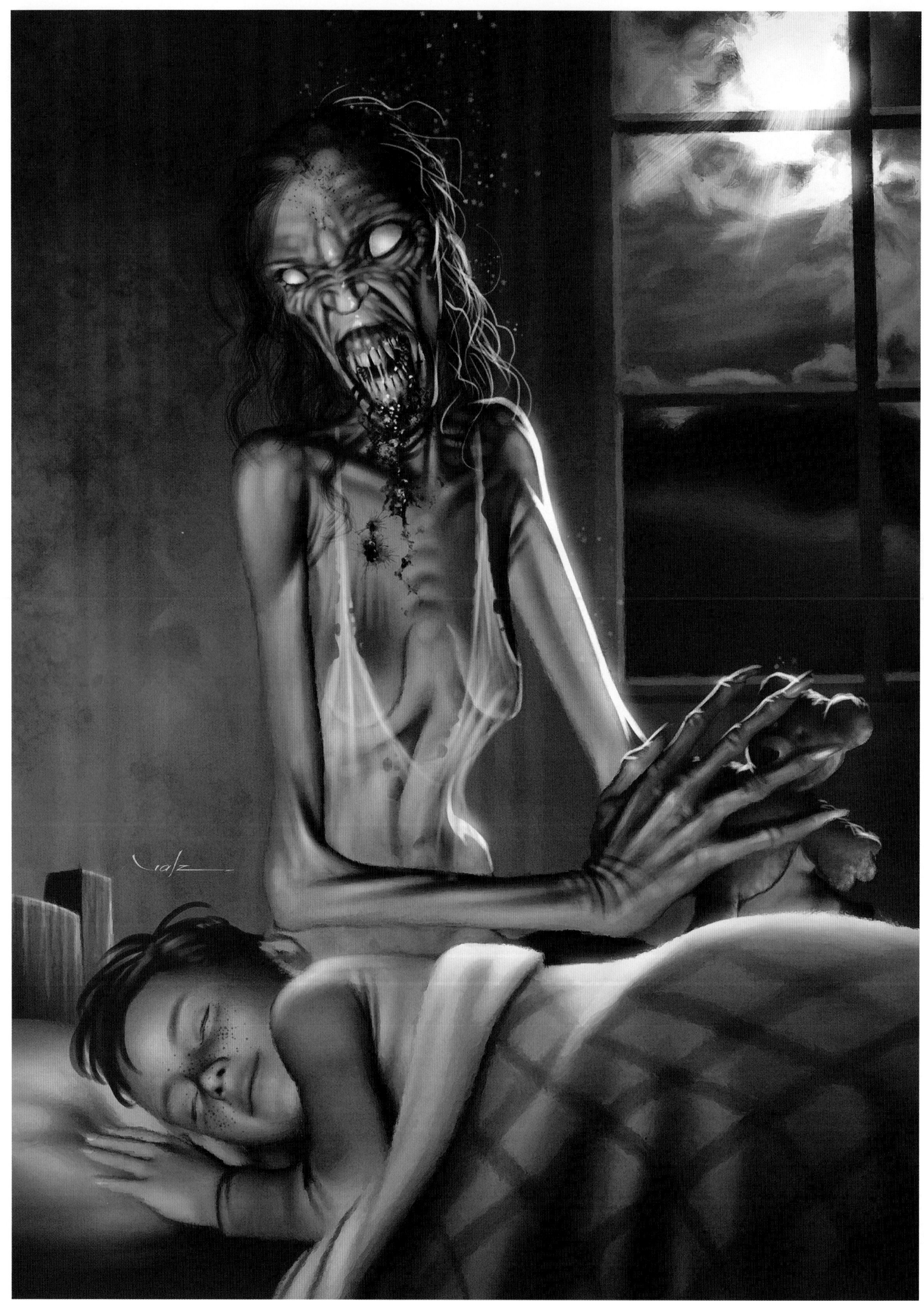

Sweet Dreams

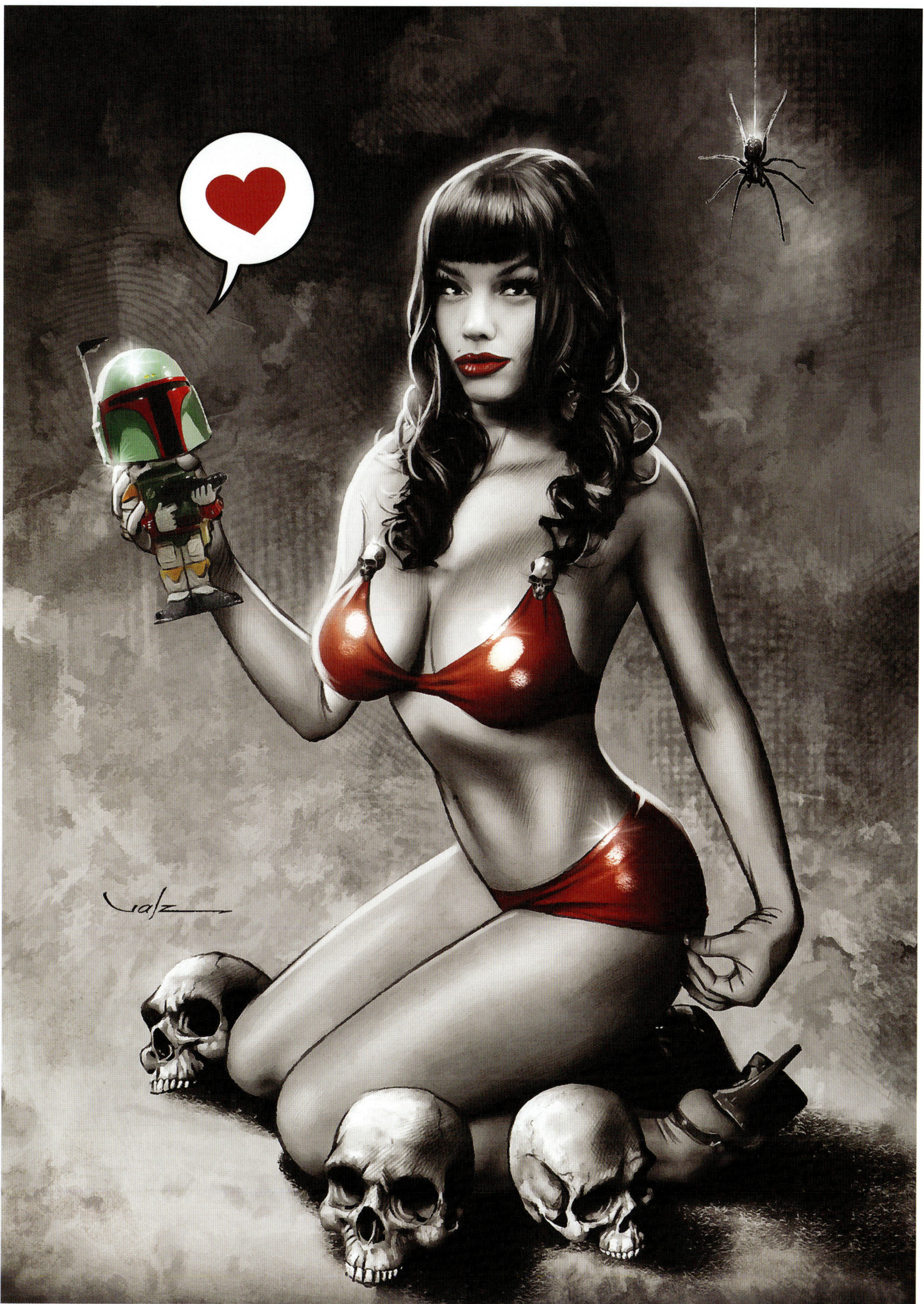
Love Naomi

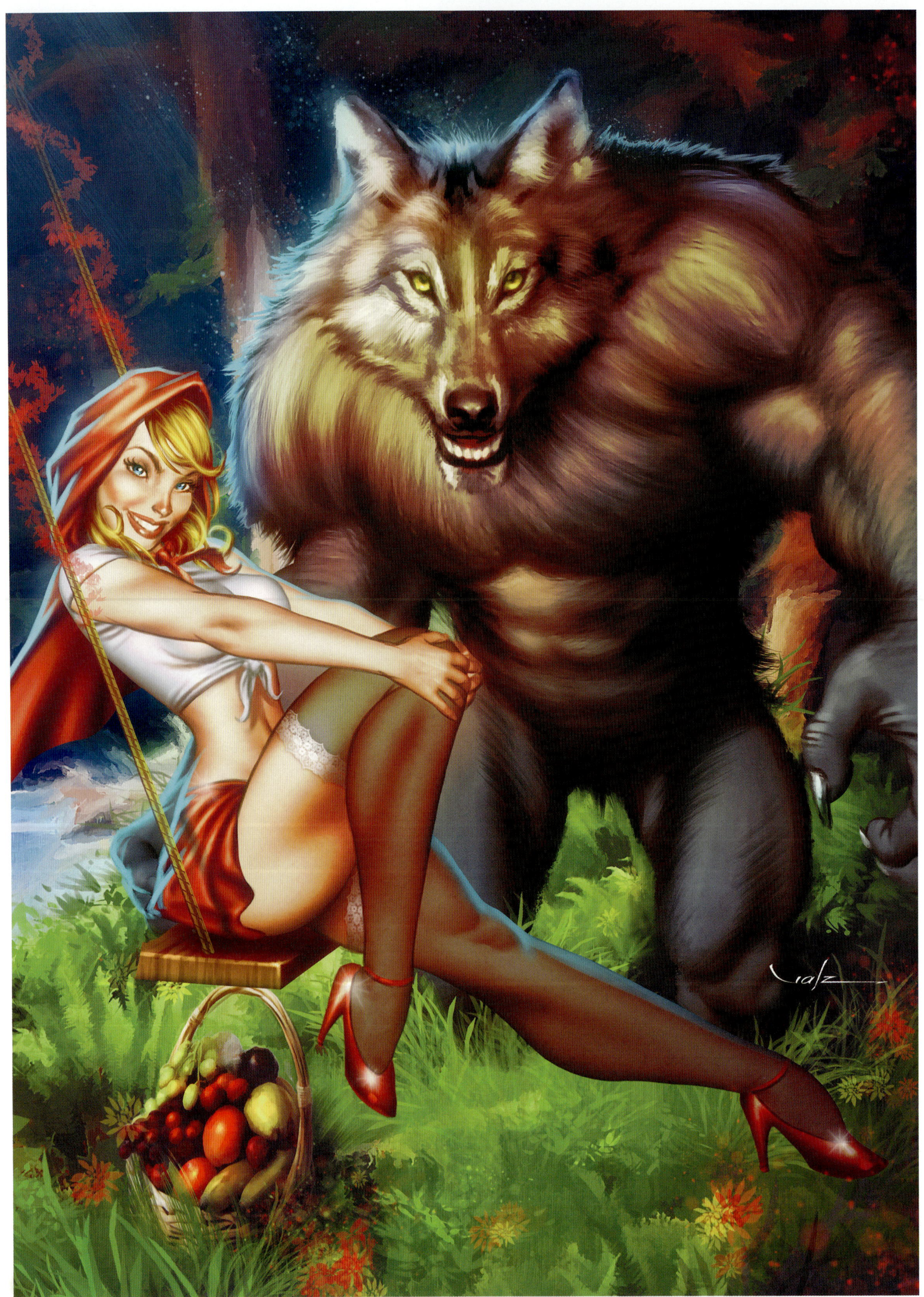

RED AND THE WOLF

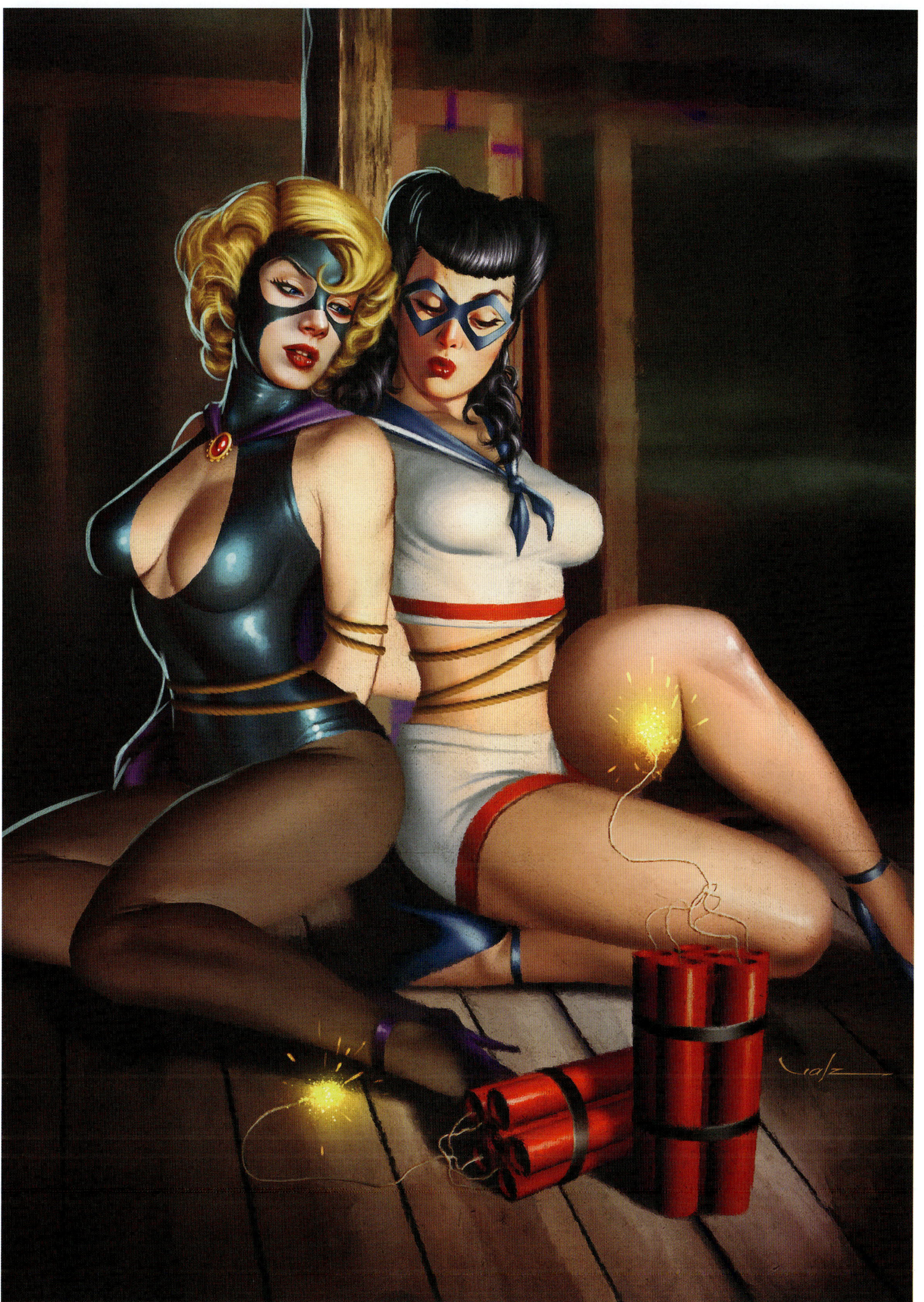

A Deadly Trap

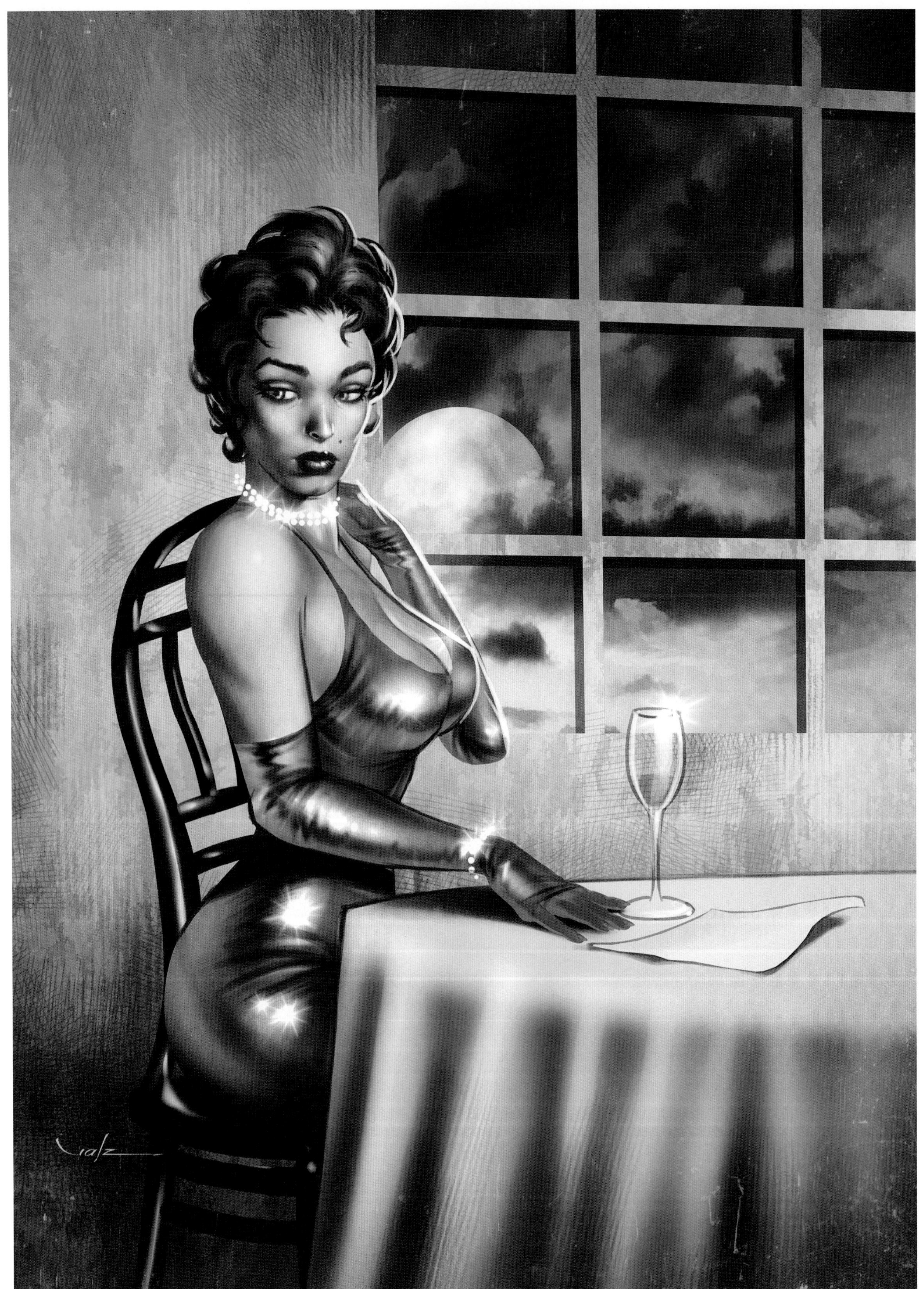

Waiting For Him

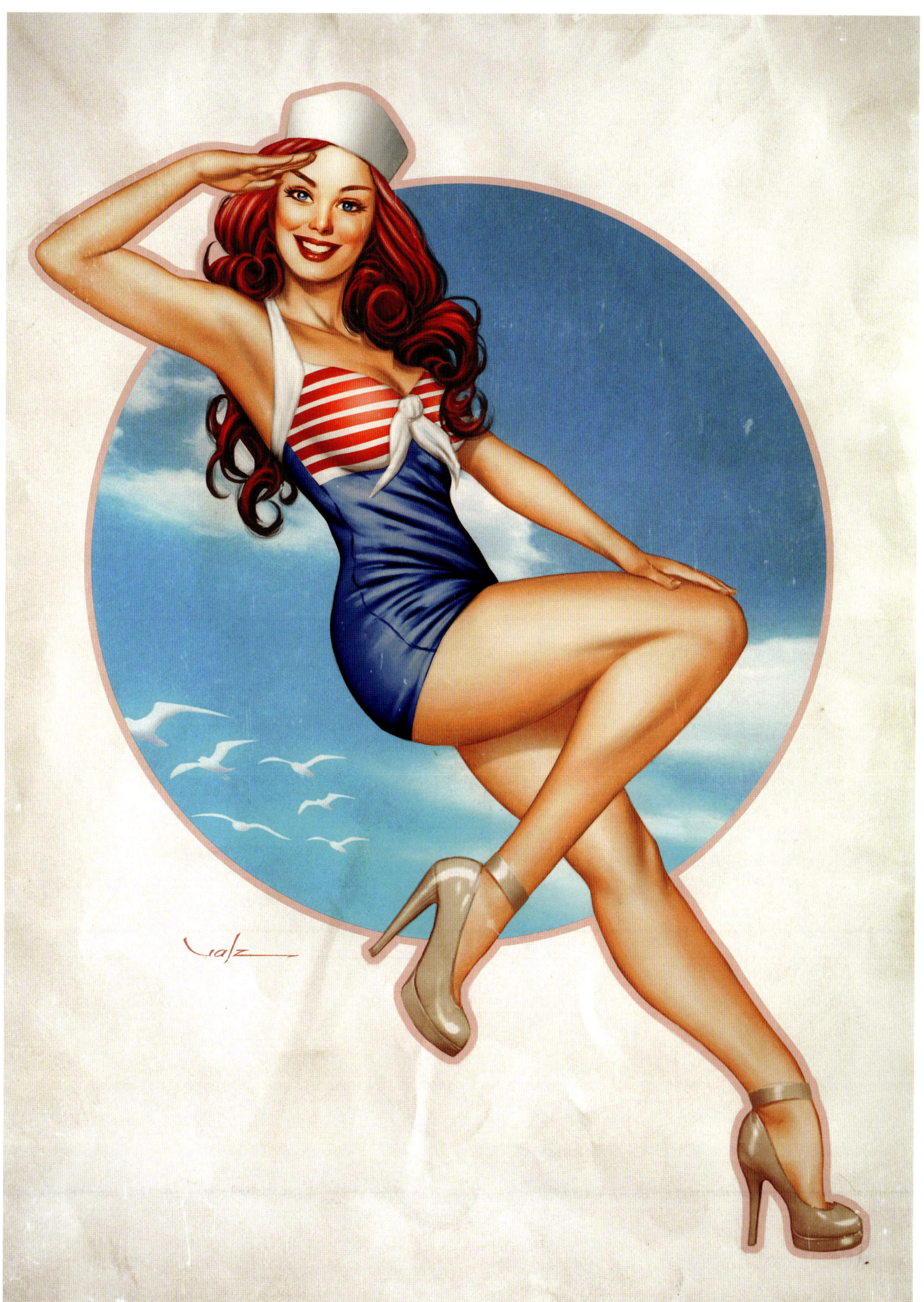

BEAUTIFUL GIRL

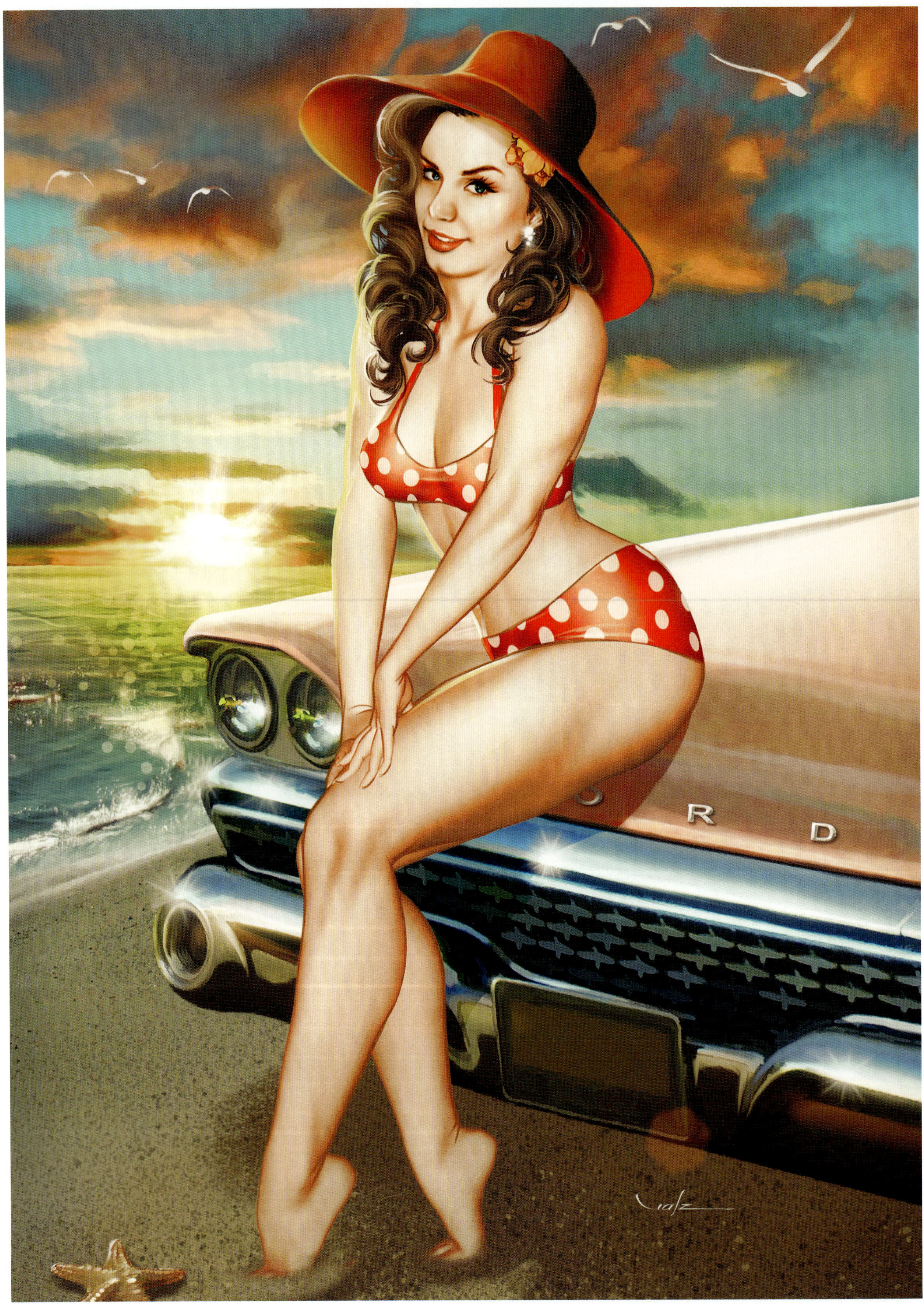

AT THE BEACH

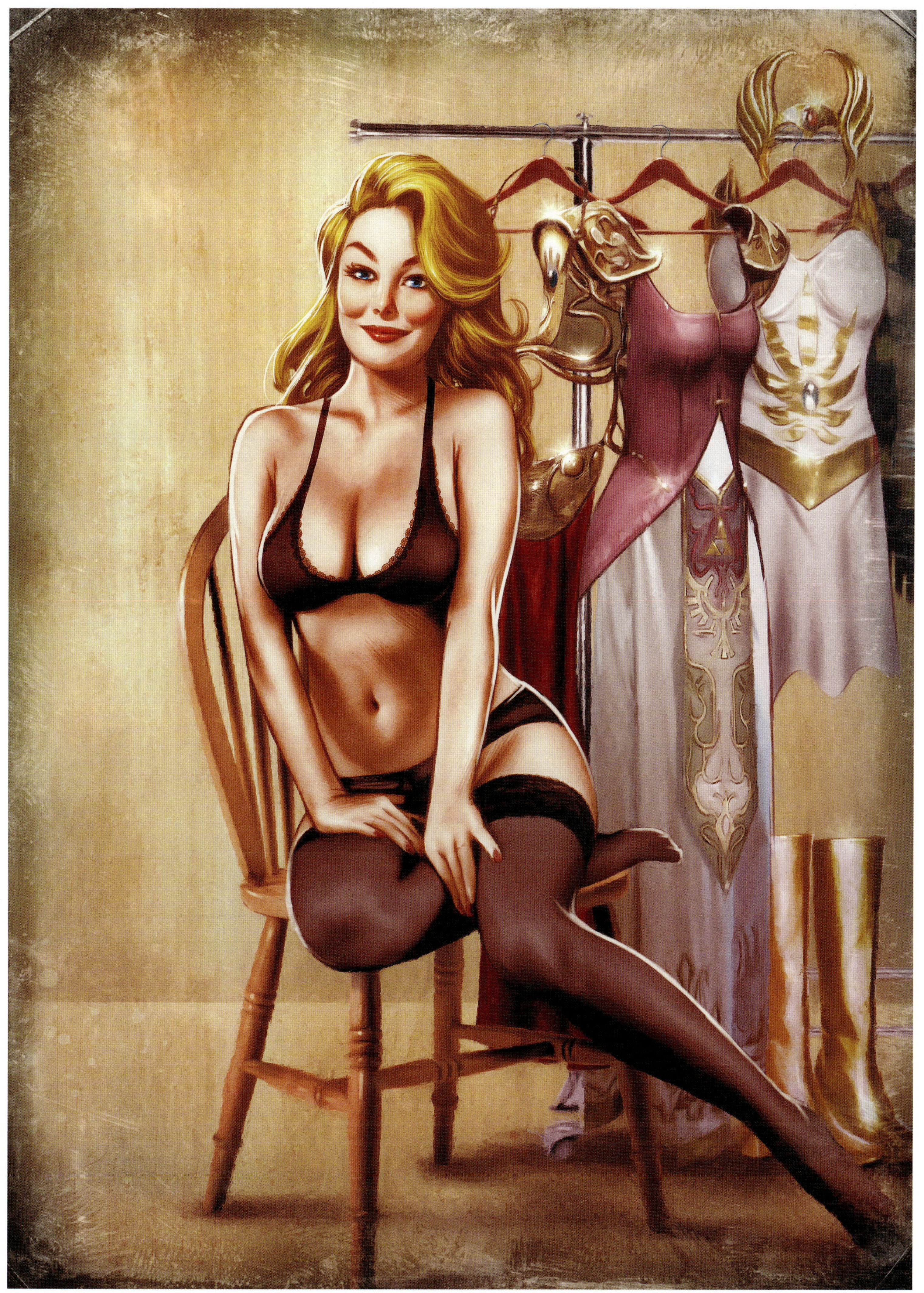

SEXY LADY

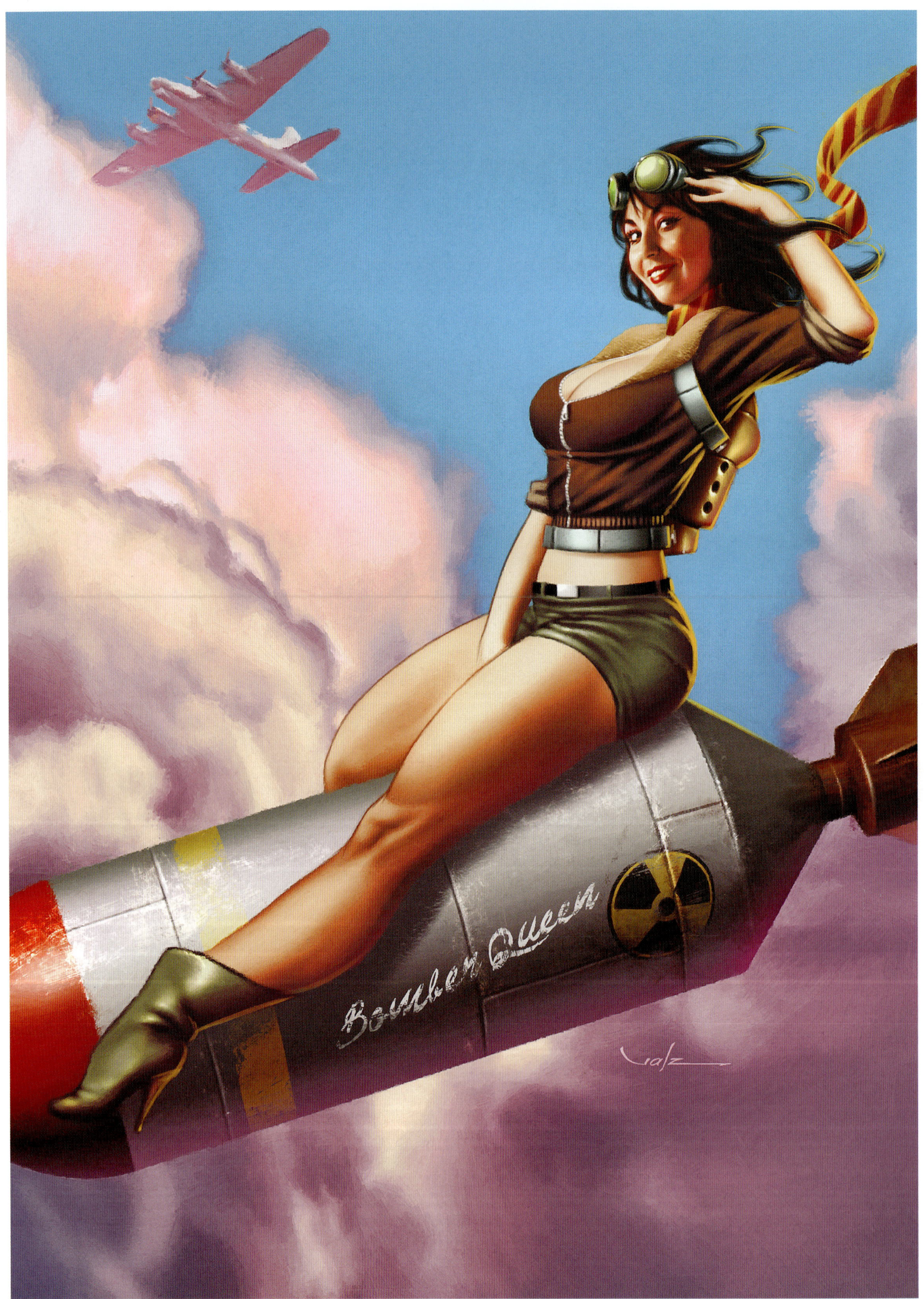

Bomber Queen